T0381161

A Journey Through Torah

An Introduction to God's Life Instructions for His Children:

Volume 5 –
D'Varim/Deuteronomy

Michael G. Wodlinger

WestBow
PRESS®
A DIVISION OF THOMAS NELSON
& ZONDERVAN

WestBow Press books may be ordered through booksellers or by contacting:

WestBow Press
A Division of Thomas Nelson & Zondervan
1663 Liberty Drive
Bloomington, IN 47403
www.westbowpress.com
844-714-3454

Interior Image Credit: Dr. Michael G. Wodlinger

ISBN: 979-8-3850-3482-6 (sc)
ISBN: 979-8-3850-3483-3 (e)

Library of Congress Control Number: 2024920439

Print information available on the last page.

WestBow Press rev. date: 10/02/2024

ACKNOWLEDGEMENTS

Glenn and Michael first acknowledge that the completion of this volume would not have happened without the guidance and leadership of ADONAI Elohim, our Lord God, to whom all praise and worship is due. We also recognize our wives, who have been with us throughout this entire process. Thank you for your patience, your support and, most of all for your love.

We acknowledge the critics, who examined the draft of the Book and have made very cogent suggestions for its improvement. We appreciate your time and effort in this task. Thank you Chantal, Flora, Joe and Reg. We are indebted to you.

And we would be remiss if we did not acknowledge you, our readers, for whom we have prepared this volume. Without you, there would be no need. Thank you.

INTRODUCTION

Whenever Kings of Israel read from Torah, the Five Books of Moses, Deuteronomy was often the book they read. Why was this Book read more than the others?

The Hebrew title of the fifth book is *D'Varim*, which means 'words' or 'utterances', focuses on an intense encapsulation of Israel's 40-year journey through the wilderness of the Sinai Peninsula. Some have called D'Varim ancient Israel's constitution[1], while others state this book serves other purposes, such as a book of instruction[2] and a summary of the covenant between ADONAI and man[3]. Indeed, as you read through this fifth volume, I am sure you will determine other purposes for this writing of *Moshe*.

Throughout the 34 chapters of the 'Book', there are a multitude of instructions, laws and regulations discussed and explained. These are not new to Israel; they are a summarization of what was given to Israel at the base of Mt. Sinai (Exodus 20) and presented within the four first books of Torah.

It does appear that *HaSefer D'Varim*, the Book of Deuteronomy, is a series of teachings or sermons given by Moshe to his people, the Congregation of ADONAI. As you read through the Book, alongside this brief introduction, keep in mind the culture of Israel at the time of its writing was much different from yours. Indeed, it was a much earlier time, with different physical challenges and much less security than we have today.

It has been suggested[4] that "The book of Deuteronomy is possibly a cornerstone to the Apostolic writings. There are numerous quotes that YESHUA and the apostles used. One may also see it as a sacred charge to the people of Israel and also a farewell address" by Moshe.

---

[1] 1.Elezar, D. J., *Deuteronomy as Israel's Ancient Constitution: Some Preliminary Reflections*, Jerusalem Centre for Public Affairs, undated, https://www.jcpa.org/dje/articles2/deut-const.htm.

[2] Miller, P.D., *Constitution or Instruction? The Purpose of Deuteronomy, Consulting the Community,* Penn State University Press, 2005.

[3] Lopez, D., *What was the purpose of Deuteronomy implied in the book for the original audience,* https://dalelopez.wordpress.com/2015/11/17/what-was-the-purpose-of-deuteronomy-implied-in-the-book-for-the-original-audience/

[4] Ducharme, R. Private conversation, February 2024.

Be aware also that there is a good deal of controversy surrounding Moshe and the writing of Torah, the five first books of the Bible. One source of controversy comes from Martin Noth[5], who claimed that there were multiple writers of the Torah. The total collection was compiled by the high priest, Ezra, who wove the stories together to create a tangible and cohesive version of Israel's life and journey through the wilderness.

STRUCTURE OF VOLUME 5: D'VARIM, DEUTERONOMY

Deuteronomy is divided into three parts: Chapters 1 to 11; 12 to 26 and 27 to 34. In the first part, Moshe calls Israel to remain faithful to ADONAI's teachings. He reminds the second generation of the faithlessness exhibited by the first. Included in this first set of teachings, are the call to action. Based on the central prayer of the Shema (Deuteronomy 6:4,5), this prayer is now central to Judaism and is recited twice a day, upon rising and retiring, and during the weekly Shabbat service.

The second section, Chapters 12 to 26, focuses on instructions and ordinances regarding worship (Deuteronomy 12 to 16a), leadership (16b to 18) and the civil life (19 to 26) of the Israelites. Through these instructions, ADONAI, through Moshe, is pushing Israel to a higher standard of society life than their neighbours. This was the highest standard of civil life than had ever been experienced before.

In Chapters 27 to 34, Moshe reviews the blessings for following ADONAI's ordinances and teachings and curses for refusing to obey. This review comes to a climax in chapter 30:15-20, when Moshe forces the issue with: *See, today I have set before you life and prosperity, death and adversity. For I am commanding you today to love the* LORD *your God, to walk in His ways, and to keep His commands, statutes, and ordinances, so that you may live and multiply . . . I call heaven and earth as witnesses against you today that I have set before you life and death, blessing and curse. Choose life so that you and your descendants may live.* This section of HaSefer D'Varim ends with Moshe's poem of warning Israel about their future (Chapter 32) and his blessings of the 12 tribes of Israel (Chapter 33). The Book then ends with Moshe's death.

The volume is further divided into *parashot*, or portions. Each *parashah*, portion, is focused on a central issue, decided by the scribes who memorized the teachings of Moshe, thousands of years ago and who eventually transcribed the Torah onto parchment scrolls. There are 11 parashot in this volume. You may read of them in the Table of Contents.

Throughout the Book, you will read transliterated Hebrew words. If they appear for the first time, they will be in a different font, such as ADONAI. Otherwise, they

---

[5] Noth, M. *The scheme of the twelve tribes of Israel*, <u>Harper Brothers</u>, New York, 1930.

will be in font used throughout the Book. Why translated Hebrew? The Book has been written through the lens of Messianic Judaism; thus, where it is appropriate, the original Hebrew word will be translated into English, instead of using its English translation. In many cases, the English translation of the Hebrew does not express the deeper meaning of the original Hebrew. Every attempt has been made to maintain the original meaning of the language used in *HaSefer D'Varim*, the Book of Deuteronomy. You will find, at the end of the Book, a glossary with all the Hebrew words fully translated.

Hello there. My name is Zakur, which in Hebrew means 'all your males shall appear'. I will be your guide through this volume. My role is to share with you some important information that may deepen your understanding.

All Scripture cited in this text originates with the Holman Christian Standard Bible, which provides in my estimation the closest meaning of the original Hebrew text. I urge you to read each of the parashah, the portions, before engaging the text of the weekly reading.

Enjoy your reading of HaSefer D'Varim, the Book of Deuteronomy.

PARASHAH D'VARIM (WORDS)

DEUTERONOMY 1:1–3:22

HASEFER D'VARIM, THE BOOK OF DEUTERONOMY IS UNIQUE IN THE TORAH, IN THAT ALL THE COMMANDS THAT MOSHE TEACHES ISRAEL HAVE BEEN GIVEN BY ADONAI ELOHIM TO ISRAEL AT THE BASE OF MT. SINAI. THE WORDS THAT MOSHE SPEAKS TO ISRAEL, UNLIKE IN THE OTHER 4 BOOKS, COME FROM MOSHE'S MOUTH, OR THE WORDS OF ADONAI, BLESSED BE HIS NAME, ORDERED HIM TO SAY, AS WE READ IN CHAPTER 1:3.

PLEASE READ THE PASSAGE FOCUSED ON HERE BEFORE YOU ENGAGE THE TEXT.

A Journey Through Torah

Parashah D'Varim (Words) Deuteronomy 1:1–3:22

Deuteronomy begins with Israel having wandered through the wilderness for 40 years. The generation that left Egypt has died; only Moshe, *Y'hoshua* and *Kalev* are still alive. As Moshe spoke to Israel, where they camped on the east side of the Yarden River, in the Aravah, they are in the first day of the 11ᵗʰ month of the 40ᵗʰ year. The month is *Adar,* on the biblical calendar, typically occurring between February and March, on the Gregorian calendar.

We are told ADONAI has defeated Sichon, king of the Emori, and Og, king of the Bashon, removing most of the competition Israel faced, when they first moved into their land.

The first chapter of this last book of Torah focuses on Moshe providing an overview of the events of the past 40 years of travel. You may notice he focuses on the negative events, which drew ADONAI's wrath and caused Israel's suffering, as we read in Deuteronomy 1:26-28: *But you were not willing to go up, rebelling against the command of the LORD your God. You grumbled in your tents and said, 'The LORD brought us out of the land of Egypt to deliver us into the hands of the Amorites so they would destroy us, because He hated us. Where can we go? Our brothers have discouraged us, saying: The people are larger and taller than we are; the cities are large, fortified to the heavens. We also saw the descendants of the Anakim there.'*

Moshe continues by recounting his selecting 70 leaders from the community, men of character and wisdom, who would address the issues emerging from day-to-day interactions. He explained that he had decided to hear only the cases that the 70 leaders could not address and, then, take those to ADONAI. You may recall, having read Exodus 18:14, when Yitro, Moshe's father-in-law, observed him and responded with: *When Moses' father-in-law saw everything he was doing for them he asked, "What is this thing you're doing for the people? Why are you alone sitting as judge, while all the people stand around you from morning until evening?* As we read in

Numbers 11:16,17, ADONAI ordered Moshe to *"Bring me seventy of Israel's elders who are known to you as leaders and officials among the people."* These were trained by ADONAI to share the burden of Moshe's leadership.

He talked to them about reaching *Kadesh-Barnea*, the hill country of the Emori. This was the place where Israel was to cross the *J* River and enter the land ADONAI gave them. However, they decided they wanted members of their community to cross over and scout-out the land for them. As we read in *HaSefer B'Midbar*, the Book of Numbers, the report brought back by the scouts was a mixture of good and bad. All the scouts spoke about the produce being rich and plentiful; however, 10 of the scouts reported that the land was populated by giants, who would devour Israel. Only *Y'hoshua* and *Kalev* attempted to rely on ADONAI's strength. You may read Kalev's impassioned speech in verses Numbers 13:30 - *"We must go up and take possession of the land because we can certainly conquer it!"* Israel wanted to stone Moshe, Y'hoshua and Kalev but ADONAI intervened and placed a plague upon the people who rebelled.

Many of the rebels decided to cross over the *Yarden* on their own, to battle the *Emori*. ADONAI warned them they would be alone; however, He was not able to dissuade them and they were badly defeated and, we assume, their numbers greatly reduced.

Chapter 2 deals with Israel's travels along the road to the Sea of Suf to the territory of the Sichon, the king of the Heshbon. Along this portion of the journey, Moshe spoke about their encountering the descendants of *Esav, Ya'akov's* brother, who lived in *Se'ir*. They were not to take any of this land, as this was given to Esav's descendants by ADONAI, as their inheritance. As they travelled through Se'ir, they were to pay for the food and water they received. These were the Edomites and were considered to be kin[6] with Israel.

As Israel travelled past the territory of Edom, they came to the desert of *Mo'av*. Moshe shared with his people that ADONAI told him they were not to engage with these people in a hostile way, as the land, called 'Ar, was given to the descendants of *Lot*, Avraham's nephew, as their inheritance. Let's read a portion of the request Moshe made to Sihon, the King of Heshbon: *So I sent messengers with an offer of peace to Sihon king of Heshbon from the Wilderness of Kedemoth, saying, [27] 'Let us travel through your land; we will keep strictly to the highway. We will not turn to the right or the left. [28] You can sell us food in exchange for silver so we may eat, and give us water for silver so we may drink. Only let us travel through on foot, [29] just as the descendants of Esau who live in Seir did for us, and the Moabites who live in 'Ar, until we cross the Jordan into the land the LORD our God is giving us.'* Deuteronomy 2:26-29.

---

[6] Encyclopedia B'ritanica https://www.B'ritannica.com/place/Edom, accessed 15 November, 2022.

We then learn that by the 38th year of their journey, all those who had joined the Exodus from Egypt had died, leaving their children and grandchildren to complete the journey. Moshe continued his narrative, telling Israel that, as they continued their journey through the Arabian Peninsula, they came to the border of Mo'av, at 'Ar. Once again, ADONAI told them not to raise arms against the people of Amon, as this was the territory given to the descendants of Lot.

However, as we read in *Sefer B'Midbar*, the Book of Numbers, as Israel was approaching the land of *Heshbon*, ruled by *Sichon*, the *Emori*, a request was sent to Sichon to allow Israel to pass through his land, paying for all the food they ate and water they drank. This request was rebuffed by Sichon and ADONAI began the process of causing distress among the peoples of Heshbon, producing great fear of Israel. Listen to His words, as recorded in verse 2: *Do not fear him, for I have handed him over to you along with his whole army and his land. Do to him as you did to Sihon king of the Amorites, who lived in Heshbon.* Numbers 21:34.

Israel advanced all along the Arnon valley, destroying all the Heshbon cities, taking cattle and booty from these cities. All their inhabitants were put to the sword. Israel could have gone further into Cana'anite territory, but Israel was told by ADONAI not to approach their distant relatives, the Ammonites, living around the *Yabok* River.

Israel then travelled north from Heshbon to the land of Bashan, ruled by Og. ADONAI again told Moshe He would put the terror into these people and Israel would easily conquer them. They took all their cities, sixty in total, their cattle and the goods, jewels etc., left within the cities.

As Israel captured the land of Heshbon, they also captured the land of the kings of the Emori east of the Yarden between the Ardon valley and Mount Hermon. These lands, including half of the land of Gilead, were cleared and turned over to the tribes of Reuben and Gad, as Moshe had promised. The half-tribe of Menashe/*M'nasheh* was given all the territory of Bashan and the remaining portion of Gilead. The leader of the half-tribe, Jair/*Yair*, was given *the entire region of Argob as far as the border of the Geshurites and Maacathites. He called Bashan by his own name, Jair's Villages.* Deuteronomy 3:14.

However, these tribes of giants were only a fraction of the total tribes within the promised land. As we read in 1 Samuel 17, the future king of Israel, David, faced such a giant Goliath, and defeated him at the valley of Elah. Then, in Judges 2, we read that Israel failed to drive out the Cana'anites from the hill country and lives among them. This interaction led to Israel's apostasy.

The three groups, Reuben, Gad and the half-tribe of Menashe, were not allowed to fully settle in the land until they had fought with the rest of Israel to unseat the Cana'anite inhabitants, west of the Yarden.

Moshe then tells his people of ADONAI's decision that *Y'hoshua*/Joshua would succeed Moshe as Israel's leader, with the assurance ADONAI would support his ventures into the new land, as we read in verse 22: *Don't be afraid of them, for the LORD your God fights for you.*

As his final comment in Chapter 3, Moshe shares his frustration and anger with Israel, as he asserts their rejection of ADONAI, over ten times, was one of the incidents that caused Moshe to lose the right to cross over into Israel's inheritance. Listen to his words, expressed in verses 23 to 26: *At that time I begged the LORD: Lord GOD, You have begun to show Your greatness and power to Your servant, for what god is there in heaven or on earth who can perform deeds and mighty acts like Yours? Please let me cross over and see the beautiful land on the other side of the Jordan, that good hill country and Lebanon. "But the LORD was angry with me on account of you and would not listen to me. The LORD said to me, 'That's enough! Do not speak to Me again about this matter.*

This is the end of our first weekly reading of Deuteronomy.

May ADONAI bless you fully and richly.

DEEPER UNDERSTANDINGS

THE ARAVAH

The Aravah is a leafy branch of the willow tree. It is one of the Four Species used during the ADONAI'S Festival of *Sukkot,* usually celebrated in May or June. The Aravah is the desert valley extending from the Dead Sea to Eilat, along Israel's border with Jordan.

ADONAI LOVES EVERYBODY

ADONAI loves everybody. It was little wonder, then, that He would want to protect those who were related, in any way, to Avraham, Yitzchak and Ya'akov. Thus, ADONAI told Israel, through Moshe, not to engage in any military way with either Edom or Mo'av. The rationale given was two-pronged. First, they were descendants via blood, the fluid of life, and then, ADONAI had protected Israel for their 40-year journey, providing all the food and water they needed and ensured their clothing did not wear-out. This, in itself, was a great miracle.

From my understanding of ADONAI's instructions to Moshe and his people, there were a vast number of people directly related to Israel, already living in the land. These were the descendants of Lot and Esav. These groups of people received ADONAI's protection, because of the covenant given to Avraham, Yitzchak and Ya'akov. Here is a clear indication of ADONAI's vast love for not only Israel but for other groups who shared Israel's values.

God loves everyone because God is fully love. What God doesn't love is sin; He cannot abide with sin.

Perhaps one of ADONAI's goals was to influence pagan nations around Israel, such that they would be drawn to deeper wisdom and understanding of ADONAI, learning and appreciating more about the faith of the Israelites and their relationship with GOD.

GIANTS IN THE LAND

If you recall, when the Israelite spies went across the Yarden, they reported observing a large group of giants occupying the land. These were *Refa'im*, who were later overtaken by the Ammonites, the descendants of *Lot*. Similarly, the *Horim*, living in *Se'ir*, were overtaken by the *Emori*, the descendants of *Esav*. We also learn that the Avim, who lived in land east of the Persian Gulf, were driven out by the Caphtorim, another peoples of giants. This was fortunate for Israel, as the Avim were extremely hostile to Israel and would have defeated them in battle.

The refusal of Israel to enter the promised land, at this point, had and continues to have a profound impact of Israel today. On the ninth day of Av, the fifth month of the Jewish calendar, all religious Jews celebrate this day as a day of fasting and prayer.

ISRAEL AND HESHBON

The story of Israel's battle with the people of Heshbon is quite interesting. ADONAI shared with Moshe, in verse 25, His desire to put fear and dread into the hearts of these people, who existed in what is now Jordan, east of Israel, in what became the home of tribe of Reuben. The fear was so great, they would have gladly capitulated, allowing Israel to take over their land and cities. At the same time, though, ADONAI persuaded the Cana'anites to resist the advance of Israel and fight to their death. Had the people of Heshbon agreed to a piece treaty with Israel, their lives would have been spared; however, they refused, and their fate was sealed.

There is a myth concerning this battle, which saw the sun stop moving through the heavens. This miracle caused great panic amongst the Cana'anites, even those far away from Heshbon, bolstering Israel's reputation as a fierce army. There was Scripture to support this miracle, found in Joshua 10:13 - *And the sun stood still and the moon stopped until the nation took vengeance on its enemies.* But was there any observed evidence?

David Sedley[7], writing an article in The Times of Israel, discovered that researchers from the University of Cambridge had identified evidence of the sun 'stopping' on October 30, 1207 BCE, the date of the oldest observed complete solar eclipse. The researchers further claim that the Hebrew description of the event, indicated the sun and the moon stopped shining, rather than stopped moving.

It appears, when Og learned of Heshbon's defeat, he immediately mobilized his forces and marched against Israel. It seems Israel had no choice but to travel north to meet this advance. Interestingly, Moshe feared Og and his armies, thus ADONAI reassured him that Israel would easily overtake them.

According to Targum Yonasan[8], Og was one of the antediluvian giants, mentioned in Genesis 6. Apparently, according to the Targum, he was the only remaining giant to survive the flood. The ruler of Heshbon, an antediluvian giant, Og or *Sichon*, was so huge he had to have an iron bed constructed for him. The bed was stored in Rabbah, with the people of Ammon. The bed measured thirteen-and-a-half feet long by six feet wide. The Ammonites retained Og's massive bed to demonstrate the overwhelming power they had to defeat Og's army.

The half tribe of Menashe volunteered to settle on the east side of the Yarden when Moshe informed the tribes of Reuben and Gad they could only settle on the eastern

---

[7] Sedley, D., *'Joshua stopped the sun' 3,224 years ago today, scientists say*, The Times of Israel, 30 October, 2017, https://www.timesofisrael.com/3224-years-later-scientists-see-first-ever-recorded-eclipse-in-joshuas-battle/ accessed 13 March, 2024.

[8] Targum Yonasan, also known as Targum Johnathan, is an Aramaic translation of the Hebrew Bible. It began as an oral translation and was transcribed as early as 5 B.C. Today the Targum is only used by Yemenite Jews, in their services.

plains only if the half-tribe joined them. Moshe believed the two tribes of Reuben and Gad would be permanently isolated from the rest of Israel. To avoid this, he split the tribe into two almost equal portions, one on the west side and the other on the east. Given that the tribes had relatives on both sides, they would have more contact with each other, allowing Reuben and Gad to maintain contact also.[9]

The village of Hovat Yair exists today in Israel, as the Yair Farm. It is a Jewish settlement in the West Bank. The land was expropriated from the arab people living there at the time and received official recognition in 2021.

MOSHE SUPPORTS Y'HOSHUA

Notice, when Moshe announced Y'hoshua would lead Israel across the Yarden River, Deuteronomy 3:21,22, he encouraged Y'hoshua with the phrase, *The LORD will do the same to all the kingdoms you are about to enter. Don't be afraid of them, for the LORD your God fights for you.* This illustrates Moshe's humility. Even though he felt let-down, because ADONAI refused to allow him to cross the Yarden, he still supported Y'hoshua's new role as Israel's leader.

Nor only did Moshe support Y'hoshua, Adonai strengthened him also and caused the people to have great regard for him.

---

[9] Rambam, also known as Maimonides, was a twelfth century Sephardic Jewish philosopher, who was the most influential Middle Ages scholar of Torah. He lived between 1138 and 1204 B.C.

Parashah Va'Etchanan

I Pleaded
Deuteronomy 3:23 to 7:11

In our second weekly reading of Torah, Moshe begins his instruction of the Torah to his people. In doing so, he focused on some of the commandments and taught others that had not been previously written.

Please read the passage focused on here before you engage the text.

Parashah Va'Etchanan

I Pleaded
Deuteronomy 3:23 to 7:11

"At that time I begged the Lord: Lord God, You have begun to show
Your greatness and power to Your servant, for what god is there in heaven
or on earth who can perform deeds and mighty acts like Yours?

Deuteronomy 3:23,24

As we begin our second weekly reading, we witness Moshe again sharing his desire to cross into the Promised Land with his people. ADONAI responded to his cry by telling him to climb to the top of Mount Pisgah and survey the land. This would be the only way Moshe could connect with Israel's new home. Notice Moshe places the blame for his situation firmly onto Israel, as we read in verse 26: *"But the Lord was angry with me on account of you and would not listen to me."*

Chapter 4 of Deuteronomy focus mainly on the need for Israel to be obedient to ADONAI's Word, as found in Torah. Read this section carefully and you may see how Moshe reiterates the covenantal relationship Israel has ADONAI.

The chapter opens with Moshe's words: *"Now, Israel, listen to the statutes and ordinances I am teaching you to follow, so that you may live, enter, and take possession of the land Yahweh, the God of your fathers, is giving you. You must not add anything to what I command you or take anything away from it, so that you may keep the commands of the Lord your God I am giving you."* Deuteronomy 4:1,2. In this instruction, Moshe reminded Israel of the experience they had with ADONAI before Mount Sinai, as we read in verse 11: *"You came near and stood at the base of the mountain, a mountain blazing with fire into the heavens and enveloped in a dense, black cloud."* This was followed by Moshe providing ADONAI's command to him

13

to teach Israel what he wanted them to know, providing a rationale for his continued leadership of them.

The second focus of Moshe's teaching deals with Israel's requirement to worship ADONAI only and in the prescribed manner. Listen to a portion of his teaching, as we read in verses 15 to 18: *"For your own good, be extremely careful -- because you did not see any form on the day the LORD spoke to you out of the fire at Horeb -- not to act corruptly and make an idol for yourselves in the shape of any figure: a male or female form, or the form of any beast on the earth, any winged creature that flies in the sky, any creature that crawls on the ground, or any fish in the waters under the earth."* Notice how Moshe ties this teaching into ADONAI's love for all peoples, with the words in verse 19(b), *The LORD your God has provided them for all people everywhere under heaven,* and naming Israel as His chosen people, as we read in verse 20: *"But the LORD selected you and brought you out of Egypt's iron furnace to be a people for His inheritance, as you are today."*

And then, Moshe returns to his often-stated anger with Israel for their rebellion against ADONAI's commands, as we read in verse 21: *"The LORD was angry with me on your account. He swore that I would not cross the Jordan and enter the good land the LORD your God is giving you as an inheritance."* This will be discussed more, below, but first recognize that Moshe committed his sin in public, displayed before the entire nation of Israel, not in private.

In the next section of chapter 4, Moshe prophesizes what will happen to Israel, when they again disobeyed ADONAI's commands, while living in their promised land. This prophecy was very accurate. Listen to what Moshe warned them, in verses 25 to 27: *"When you have children and grandchildren and have been in the land a long time, and if you act corruptly, make an idol in the form of anything, and do what is evil in the sight of the LORD your God, provoking Him to anger, I call heaven and earth as witnesses against you today that you will quickly perish from the land you are about to cross the Jordan to possess. You will not live long there, but you will certainly be destroyed. The LORD will scatter you among the peoples, and you will be reduced to a few survivors among the nations where the LORD your God will drive you."* We read of this conquest of Israel in 2 Kings 17. However, Moshe leaves his people with a comforting word of ADONAI's love, as we read in verse 31: *"He will not leave you, destroy you, or forget the covenant with your fathers that He swore to them by oath, because the LORD your God is a compassionate God."* Not wanting to leave his people with a bad taste in their mouths, Moshe outlined specific instances of ADONAI's display of love for His people.

There is something I find quite intriguing about this portion of Chapter 4; even though Israel has disobeyed ADONAI many times, He maintains a strong loving relationship with His people. This, I believe is related to the covenant He cut with Avraham, Yitzchak and Ya'akov, the patriarchs of Israel.

In Deuteronomy 5, Moshe outlines the covenant Israel agreed to, when they stood at the foot of Mt. Sinai, 38 years earlier. In this section of Torah, Moshe reiterates the contents of the covenant, the Ten Commandments. This was his teaching their fathers received on that day. I draw your attention to verses 12 to 15, the section outlining Shabbat. Read this passage, below:

Be careful to remember the Sabbath day, to keep it holy as the LORD your God has commanded you. You are to labor six days and do all your work, but the seventh day is a Sabbath to the LORD your God. You must not do any work—you, your son or daughter, your male or female slave, your ox or donkey, any of your livestock, or the foreigner who lives within your gates, so that your male and female slaves may rest as you do. Remember that you were a slave in the land of Egypt, and the LORD your God brought you out of there with a strong hand and an outstretched arm. That is why the LORD your God has commanded you to keep the Sabbath day.

Notice that Moshe taught this group that even their slaves (servants) are to take the Shabbat as a day of rest. If they, the owners, remember they were once slaves in Egypt, they will more easily remember to allow their servants to rest.

It might be important to remember the covenant ADONAI made with Avraham, Yitzchak and Ya'akov. In this covenant, ADONAI clearly outlined His love for His people and how He would lead them to the land He had set aside for them. His covenant also displays His steadfast love for Israel and His unilateral decision never to totally abandon them. Yes, He was clear that He would discipline them and this He did several times, throughout the years. His devoted love would always remain with His people.

Notice that Moshe doesn't seek further reassurance of Israel's acceptance of their covenant, rather he reiterates the acceptance their fathers gave and reminded this new generation of their responsibility to carry out ADONAI's commands. Listen to his precise words: *Be careful to do as the LORD your God has commanded you; you are not to turn aside to the right or the left. 33 Follow the whole instruction the LORD your God has commanded you, so that you may live, prosper, and have a long life in the land you will possess.* Deuteronomy 5:32, 33.

As you read further, into verses 24 to 27, observe carefully how Moshe shares how the previous generation desired him to be their intermediary with ADONAI. Their key rationale seems to be, *But now, why should we die? This great fire will consume us and we will die if we hear the voice of the Lord our God any longer,* as we read in verse 25. The reasons for Moshe to assume this role are discussed below.

Chapter 6 introduces us to one of the most powerful prayer for Jews and Messianic believers – the Shema, meaning <u>listen and obey</u>. Said every morning and evening, the Shema helps remind us of ADONAI's presence with us. Let's look at it carefully:

> *Listen, Israel: The LORD our God, the LORD is One.*
> *Love the LORD your God with all your heart, with*
> *all your soul, and with all your strength.*
> *These words that I am giving you today are to be in your heart.*
> *Repeat them to your children.*
> *Talk about them when you sit in your house and when you walk*
> *along the road, when you lie down and when you get up.*
> *Bind them as a sign on your hand and let them be a symbol on your*
> *forehead. Write them on the doorposts of your house and on your gates.*
> Deuteronomy 6:4-9

The next portion of Chapter 6 focuses on Moshe teaching his people to remember (keep in their hearts, and act with their hands, feet and lips) ADONAI through obeying His commands. Moshe does this by informing them of what they will assume, when they enter the promised land. Read this section carefully and notice what they will receive: *a land with large and beautiful cities that you did not build, houses full of every good thing that you did not fill them with, wells dug that you did not dig, and vineyards and olive groves that you did not plant—and when you eat and are satisfied.* Deuteronomy 6: 10,11.

This is followed by Moshe's exhortation to follow ADONAI's teaching through all their lives, remembering His love for them, and prospering in the land He has given Israel, as we read in verse 18: *Do what is right and good in the Lord's sight, so that you may prosper and so that you may enter and possess the good land the Lord your God swore to give your fathers.*

Chapter 6 ends with Moshe's command for parents to teach their children the history of their people, beginning with the exodus. He finishes with the very poignant phrase, *Righteousness will be ours if we are careful to follow every one of these commands before the Lord our God, as He has commanded us.* Deuteronomy 6:25.

The short portion of chapter 7, at the end of this week's reading, presents Israel with a command to have no relations with the inhabitants of the land they are to conquer. We understand this clearly in verse 2: *and when the LORD your God delivers them over to you and you defeat them, you must completely destroy them. Make no treaty with them and show them no mercy.* ADONAI wants His people to be devoted to Him entirely, keeping the land clean, i.e. pure, with no temptation upon Israel. We read of His creation of Israel as His people in verse 6: *For you are a holy people belonging to the LORD your God. The LORD your God has chosen you to be His own possession out of all the peoples on the face of the earth.*

This is the end of our weekly reading.

May ADONAI bless you fully and richly.

DEEPER UNDERSTANDINGS

MOSHE'S COMPLAINT

Unable to release his disappointment with ADONAI's refusal to allow him to cross the Yarden, Moshe once more raises his complaint. Although he was a very humble man (Numbers 12:3), he was nevertheless human. He cared about his people, and he wanted to ensure their safe crossing of the Yarden River. Does this mean he didn't trust ADONAI to ensure their safe crossing? Human desires are more complex than we may realize. Yes, Moshe trusted ADONAI and, at the same time, he felt responsible for their safety, as their leader. As with many leaders, he had difficulty releasing himself from that responsibility. Thus, he returned again to ADONAI and pressed Him further.

Why did he blame Israel for ADONAI's refusal? As you followed Israel's serial betrayals of ADONAI's commands, you may have noticed Moshe's frame of mind, as he responded to each. It appears that at Kadesh, Israel's complaints about the lack of water, struck a nerve with Moshe. As we have read in Numbers 20:7,8, ADONAI told him: *"Take the staff and assemble the community. You and your brother Aaron are to* speak to the rock *while they watch, and it will yield its water. You will bring out water for them from the rock and provide drink for the community and their livestock."*

(emphasis added). Notice, then, Moshe's anger, as he did not speak to the rock but struck it, twice, as we read in verse 10: *"Listen, you rebels! Must we bring water out of this rock for you?"* Why would this have upset ADONAI? By having Moshe speak to the rock, ADONAI was ensuring Israel realized that it was ADONAI, not Moshe, who supplied them with water. When Moshe struck the rock, he usurped ADONAI and assumed His power. For ADONAI, this was unforgivable and, as a consequence, he refused to allow Moshe to lead His people across the Yarden River. So, it appears, if Israel had not complained again to Moshe, questioning ADONAI's love for them, Moshe would not have been in the situation he was.

Moshe's humility was emphasized by Adonai. However, he had an insecurity about his leadership and felt inadequate to meet his people's needs.

ISRAEL MUST OBEY ADONAI

The rationale for this commandment lies in the reality of Israel living within a foreign land, whose peoples do not know ADONAI. If Israel is to fulfill the function given to them as ADONAI's nation of priests (Exodus 19:6), they must demonstrate their allegiance to Him and faithfully obey His commands. This generation is not those who escaped Egypt; these are the children of that group. They have only known

ADONAI's loving kindness for them, one of His attributes, as He has travelled with them as a cloud during the day and fire at night. Through his teachings, Moshe was attempting to develop within Israel their understanding that their success, as an invading nation, fully depended on their adherence to ADONAI's commands. By using the phrase, *Your eyes have seen what the LORD did at Baal-peor,* Moshe was personalizing the experience for even the youngest of Israel.

ADONAI realized Israel was travelling through and would be living in lands occupied by pagans. By following His commands, consistently, those around Israel would observe examples of the inherent wisdom within the commands and convince Israel of the Divine wisdom within ADONAI's decrees.

Why did Moshe emphasize Israel's experience at Mt. Sinai, as noted in Exodus 19 and 20? Many of the people present at the time of this teaching were not yet born. By reiterating Israel's experience, they would be able to testify to the giving of Torah, even if they were not there. To accomplish this, they were to share the events of Sinai with every new generation.

Was Moshe Shirking his responsibility?

Many commentators[10] criticize Moshe for transferring his responsibility for sinning before ADONAI to Israel. At first reading of Deuteronomy 3:26, we find his concern expressed as: *But the LORD was angry with me on account of you and would not listen to me.* There are other commentators who find Moshe was actually teaching Israel in love. Which approach is more accurate? Let's examine this question in some detail.

In the Talmud[11] we find the following comment, *Hakadosh Baruch Hu said to Moses: By what right do you wish to enter? It is like a shepherd who loses the flock of the king... God said to Moses: Your reputation is that you brought 600,000 (Israelites out of Egypt) and buried them in the wilderness. Now you wish to lead a new generation?* This section of analysis suggests that Moshe's actions as the leader of Israel has run its course. Could it be that, after leading Israel for 40 years, Moshe has lost his leadership skills?

Rabbi Medan[12], writing about Moshe's leadership states, *it was his failure in his*

---

[10] See, for example, Gass, A., *The sin of Moses*, Church of Christ, Columbus, Texas, 14 February, 2020. https://westoakschurchofchrist.com/articles/2020/02/14/the-sin-of-moses-what-happened-at-meribah, accessed 09 January, 2024.

[11] Bamidbar Rabba 19:13

[12] Rabbi Ya'akov Medan, an Orthodox rabbi, living in Israel.

response to the Spies that was Moses (sic) *failure. He should have publicly denounced their report, he should have argued and silenced them.*

Rabbi Alex Israel, writing in "Thinking Torah," states, *He could have changed his fate. But he acted in the same manner as he had acted earlier; a stance of passivity, turning to God, away from the people. He had not corrected his leadership flaw. He could not continue to lead. Notice how the verse says not that he may not enter Canaan, but rather that he may not "lead the congregation." His flaw was a leadership flaw.*[13] This criticism is quite clear; Moshe had the opportunity to correct his error, when he faced the spies and their biased report, at Meribah. However, he acted in the same manner, refusing to confront Israel with their lack of faith and, instead, going right to ADONAI.

Moshe felt that he was inadequate to lead Israel and asked ADONAI to take over the leadership of His people.

But, what about other positions? Rabbi Abravanel, a well respected rabbi and philosopher in 15th Century Portugal, explained, *When, in Parshat Chukat, the people complained regarding the lack of water, and they mentioned, in the course of their complaint, that Moshe and Aharon had caused the nation to be in this situation - the death in the desert and their restriction from entering the Land — "Why did you bring*

---

[13] Rabbi Alex Israel, *Thinking Torah*, https://www.alexisrael.org/devarim---moses-accusation, 2001.

the community of God to the desert to die, us and our flocks" (Bamidbar 20:5) – then the Torah records how Moshe and Aharon went into the Tent of Meeting in a state of shame and embarrassment... then God commanded them to perform the action of bringing forth water. Moshe got angry with the people ... and God was furious with Moses ...at this point God gave them the punishment for their earlier sin. Mei Meriva was just the trigger; it was not the primary cause.[14] Abravanel's perception is quite intriguing. It does agree with others', who see ADONAI's punishment of Moshe as a result of his few errors in judgment.

ADONAI's LOVE FOR ISRAEL

Perhaps you have developed the impression that ADONAI was losing patience with Israel, since they argued and rebelled against Him so often. However, imagine a loving parent; does he or she stop loving their children when they argue and rebel against their parents? Some do, of course; however, these are in the minority. Most realize their children are going through a phase and will grow out of their rebellious phase.

Remember, ADONAI is the perfect parent; He became frustrated with His children's behaviour, as we have read in Numbers 13, Judges 2 and Jeremiah 3. However, He brought them back to Him each time. ADONAI's love is more. In Hebrew, love is אַהֲבָה, ahavah, and it carries with it the connotation of loving kindness, steadfast bonding, covenant commitment and intimate friendship. His love for us is not diminished by how we treat Him. Yes, He will discipline us if we do rebel, as any loving parent would. Remember, though, He is the perfect Parent, so His love is much stronger, deeper and covenantal than any human being could love.

REMEMBERING

Like all Hebrew verbs, the verb 'to remember', זָכַר, zakar, involves action. Unlike the English translation, which is based on a Greek mindset, the Hebrew verb requires us to do something when we remember. For example, when I say to my wife "I remembered your birthday, it means I have done something in response to my mind having recalled the date and the event. So I have bought her a present and have made a reservation for dinner.

When Moshe tells Israel to remember the commandments given to them by ADONAI, he means walk them out throughout their lives. They are not only to keep them in their minds and their hearts but to make them active in their lives.

14

You may consider the word 'remember' as a plough creating a furrow through your brain; what you are to do is always there in your brain. It must be done. Remember what Adonai YESHUA said, as recorded in Yochanan (John) 14:15 – "If you love Me, you will keep My commands." In order to keep His commands, we must know (observe, guard, obey) them. They are all found in Torah.

ISRAEL'S APOSTASY AND DESTRUCTION

We find Moshe's first prophecy of Israel's capture by Assyria, brought about by their apostasy. It is important to note a more positive predictive statement, as we read in verses 29 to 31 of Chapter 4. Clearly, ADONAI put this prophecy into Moshe's mind and encouraged him to share it with Israel. However, through the following generations, they did not heed Moshe's words and, soon after settling in their promised land, lapsed into worshipping other gods and idols.

The prophecy does appear quite harsh, describing they're being scattered throughout the world and worshipping foreign deity. We discover this to be quite true, even into our current time. Notice, in verse 32, Moshe uses the 'path' analogy (*you are not to turn aside to the right or the left*). Deuteronomy 5:32. This becomes a prime symbol for those who desire to follow ADONAI and walk with Him and *ADONAI YESHUA*, the LORD JESUS.

However, there is hope that His people will be drawn together in Israel and will flourish, as they turn to ADONAI and approach Him as their only God. We are told in Zechariah 14:4, *On that day His feet will stand on the Mount of Olives, which faces Jerusalem on the east. The Mount of Olives will be split in half from east to west, forming a huge valley, so that half the mountain will move to the north and half to the south.* This is only the entry into a much larger prophecy, which outlines for us the return of ADONAI YESHUA.

THE COVENANT REVISITED

Moshe saw his role, not only as leader but also, as teacher. In this chapter of Deuteronomy, he is reiterating the teaching ADONAI had given Israel, when they stood before Him at Mt. Sinai. Unfortunately, they had difficulty adhering to His commands and, thus, died along the route. Thus, Israel needed to hear ADONAI's commands again, this time from their human teacher. As well as reminding Israel of the agreement their ancestors reached with ADONAI, Moshe also taught them the contents of the Covenant – the Ten Commandments, aseret hadevarim, הַדְּבָרִים עֲשֶׂרֶת, Ten Words in Hebrew.

You may have noticed Moshe's statement, at the beginning of Chapter 5, *He did not make this covenant with our fathers, but with all of us who are alive here today.* What does this mean? Moshe's reference to *all of us who are alive here today*, refers to all who are reading this chapter today, if they see themselves as being part of or associated with Israel, being grafted-in.

You may also have noticed a difference between Moshe's reiteration of the Ten Commandments here in Deuteronomy and how they were expressed in Exodus 20. In Exodus 20, ADONAI was teaching the first generation of Israel the instructions, as He crafted them. In Deuteronomy 5, Moshe is teaching the second generation of Israelites in a way they could best understand.

In his teaching, Moshe insisted that Israel's slaves and servants were also to keep the Shabbat as a day of rest. Why was this emphasized? During this period of time, there were no days of rest, for anyone. Slaves worked seven days a week, until they died. Thus, realizing that a day of rest is crucial for everyone's longevity, the Shabbat was instituted. But why were animals given a day of rest?

In His infinite wisdom, ADONAI knew that if animals worked everyday of the week, their owners or drivers did also. So, in order to ensure everyone rested on this day, He insisted that animals rested also.

When is the Shabbat? This is a question that has been debated for centuries. Is it

Saturday, as Jews and Messianic believers (and others) insist it is, or is it the first day of the week, Sunday, the accepted day of the Lord, ADONAI YESHUA'S original day of resurrection? Scripture tells us Shabbat is the seventh day of the week. This means we count from the first day, which is Sunday. Well, how did the Shabbat change from Saturday to Sunday? To answer this question, we need to go back into the history of Christianity to March 7, 321 CE, when Constantine issued the following decree: *All judges and city people and the craftsmen shall rest on the venerable day of the sun. Country people, however, may freely attend to the cultivation of the fields, because it frequently happens that no other days are better adapted for planting the grain in the furrows or the vines in trenches. So that the advantage given by heavenly providence may not for the occasion of a short time perish.*[15][10] Thus, from that day onward, Shabbat was held on Sundays, within Christian communities and beyond.

In an undated letter, James Gibbons, the archbishop of Baltimore in the early 20th Century, emphatically stated, *Is Saturday the seventh day according to the Bible and the Ten Commandments? I answer yes. Is Sunday the first day of the week and did the Church change the seventh day -Saturday - for Sunday, the first day? I answer yes . Did Christ change the day'? I answer no! Faithfully yours, J. Card. Gibbons*[16]. Yes, the debate will surely continue.

MOSHE AS ISRAEL'S CONNECTION TO ADONAI

I try to imagine what it must have been like for Israel, standing before Mount Sinai, with the whole mountain shrouded in smoke and the mountain top blazing with holy fire. How terrified they must have been. We receive an inkling of their fear, as we read verses 24 and 25 of Chapter 5: *'Look, the LORD our God has shown us His glory and greatness, and we have heard His voice from the fire. Today we have seen that God speaks with a person, yet he still lives. But now, why should we die? This great fire will consume us and we will die if we hear the voice of the LORD our God any longer'.* The first generation of Israel, who escaped from Egypt, still had great fear of ADONAI's power and refused to accept their new role.

Moshe didn't usurp Israel's role as the people who should speak directly to ADONAI; Israel gave him that role. Note their plea, as we found in verse 27: *'Go near and listen to everything the Lord our God says. Then you can tell us everything*

---

[15] A civil decree from Constantine I, the emperor of Rome.

[16] Gibbons, J. Card., *The faith of our Fathers*, The Catholic Mirror, Vol. 88, p. 89, 1893.

the Lord our God tells you; we will listen and obey'. Thus, Moshe became Israel's intermediary with Israel.

THE SHEMA

As mentioned above, the *Shema* (Deuteronomy 6:4) is the quintessential prayer recited by Jewish people and Messianic believers when they wake up in the morning and when they retire at night. The prayer begins with the requirement for Israel, natural and grafted-in, to listen and obey ADONAI's Words. The word Shema, in Hebrew, means listen and obey.

The second statement, *The Lord our God, the Lord is One,* Deuteronomy 6:5, is rather unique, in that the word used for *One* in this verse is אֶחָד, *echad,* rather than the usual word for one, אַחַת, *achat.* However, echad doesn't mean one, literally. The usual meaning of this word refers to a single entity, focusing on unity of more than one, composed of many parts. For Messianic believers, this provides proof of ADONAI being the Father, Son and the Holy Spirit.

The third statement, *Love the Lord your God with all your heart, with all your soul, and with all your strength,* Deuteronomy 6:5, commands us to hold ADONAI close in our hearts, in our souls, with all our might and work out this love through our actions. This reminds us of His connection to His chosen people. As usual, the verb love requires action in the form of doing something to show love, in this case, obey His commands.

The fourth statement, *These words that I am giving you today are to be in your heart,* Deuteronomy 6:6, commands us to be conscious of His love with us at all times. This is an extremely important concept, as the pressures of the world tend to want to move us further away from Him.

Then we find the first teaching commandment, *Repeat* (teach) *them to your children.* Deuteronomy 6:7. As His people are to teach Torah to the nations, as we read earlier, they must begin in their homes, encouraging them to carry on the roles of their parents.

This is followed by, *Talk about them when you sit in your house and when you walk along the road, when you lie down and when you get up.* Deuteronomy 6:7b. Here we find the second teaching command. We are to be discussing ADONAI's Word with everyone we meet, either in the house or outside. This is how we teach Torah, spreading His Word around the world.

Finally, we come to the commandment that tells us to walk our talk, *Bind them as a sign on your hand and let them be a symbol on your forehead. Write them on the doorposts of your house and on your gates.* Deuteronomy 6:8,9. Teachers around the world know their students will follow their leadership fully, when they see their teachers doing what they teach. Hypocrisy emerges as the obvious folly of doing something other than what we are teaching our students, or others, to do.

ISRAEL ARE ADONAI'S PEOPLE

In telling Israel that they are ADONAI's people, Moshe is sharing with them ADONAI does not rely on a human rationale for a king accepting the most abundant population to be his nation. By choosing them, ADONAI is showing He found something in them that was uniquely meritorious[17]. Do you find this to be a bit arrogant? There was nothing about ancient Israel that was meritorious. They were arrogant, hard-hearted and self-willed. It is my opinion that these were the reasons He chose them, because they could be developed into the nation who eventually would teach the world how to observe Torah.

In using the contents of verse 8, Moshe displayed two distinctives. The first is ADONAI found Israel to be precious and, therefore, worthy of His love and, second, ADONAI knew their love for Him would be steadfast, through the love their patriarchs felt for ADONAI. These two reasons created for ADONAI a friend who would remain loyal, no matter what the obstacles in their path[18].

However, Moshe clearly warns Israel to stay on their current path, following ADONAI. Failure to do so will result in their being refused admission to His Kingdom, where their full reward will be received.

This completes the explanations of our second weekly reading.
May the God of Abraham, Isaac and Jacob bless you fully and richly.

---

[17] Ramban, as found in Scherman, N and Zlotowitz, M., Eds. *The chumash*, <u>Menorah Publications</u>, 2000, p 978.
[18] Ramban, Ibid.

Parashah Ekev (Because)

Deuteronomy 7:12 to 11:25

In our third weekly reading, Moshe continues, in his teaching to Israel, encouraging the people to conquer the land and receive vast blessings in all aspects of their lives.

Please read the passage focused on here before you engage the text.

Parashah Ekev (Because)

Deuteronomy 7:12 to 11:25

Be careful to follow these statutes and ordinances in the land that Yahweh, the God of your fathers, has given you to possess all the days you live on the earth.

Deuteronomy 7:12

In this, our third weekly reading, Moshe continues his teaching of the children of Israel, warning them about the inhabitants of the land they are occupying. He told them to rid the land of the false idols and their worship sites – sacred pillars, *Asherah* poles, sacred poles or trees standing near Cana'anite religious places, and carved images. Moshe also warned them not to intermarry with their daughters or sons, as this would pull them into the idolatry that would destroy Israel. The rationale for these warnings is to be found in verse 6: *For you are a holy people belonging to the LORD your God. The LORD your God has chosen you to be His own possession out of all the peoples on the face of the earth.*

As we venture into Deuteronomy 8, we are met with Moshe's admonishment of Israel to hold onto ADONAI's commands and to remember what He did for them the past 40 years. We read this in verses 1 to 3 - *You must carefully follow every command I am giving you today, so that you may live and increase, and may enter and take possession of the land the LORD swore to your fathers. Remember that the LORD your God led you on the entire journey these 40 years in the wilderness, so that He might humble you and test you to know what was in your heart, whether or not you would keep His commands. He humbled you by letting you go hungry; then He gave you manna to eat, which you and your fathers had not known, so that you might learn that man does not live on bread alone but on every word that comes from the mouth of the LORD.* Moshe provides three key examples of ADONAI's blessing Israel throughout this time: He allowed them to be hungry, their first month in the wilderness, for them to realize they were dependent on Him for all their food, and <u>then</u> gave them manna to assuage their hunger; their clothes did not wear out, including their sandals, and their feet did not swell, with all the heat and walking.

Moshe continues his teaching with the promises ADONAI has given him, namely Israel would find their new land abounded with source of good water, rich soil to grow a multitude of crops and opportunities to mine iron and copper. He concludes this portion of his teaching with the words: *When you eat and are full, you will praise the Lord your God for the good land He has given you.* Deuteronomy 8:10.

Moshe's main concern seems to be Israel would forget their allegiance to ADONAI and begin worshipping other gods, made of wood, stone clay or metal. Notice the tone within the words he spoke - *Be careful that you don't forget the Lord your God by failing to keep His command -- the ordinances and statutes -- I am giving you today.* Deuteronomy 8:11. After recounting all the blessings they have received from ADONAI, during their journey through the wilderness, Moshe warns Israel of their predilection to assume they are the source of their strength, not ADONAI. Listen to his plea - *You may say to yourself, 'My power and my own ability have gained this wealth for me,' but remember that the Lord your God gives you the power to gain wealth, in order to confirm His covenant He swore to your fathers, as it is today.* Deuteronomy 8: 17,18. He completes this portion of his teaching with the warning, *Like the nations the Lord is about to destroy before you, you will perish if you do not obey the Lord your God.* Deuteronomy 8:20.

Chapter 9 begins with Moshe's encouraging words to Israel, reminding them of ADONAI's support in their upcoming battles with the Cana'anites they will face, when they cross the Jordan River. Listen to his words - *The people are strong and tall, the descendants of the Anakim. You know about them and you have heard it said about them, 'Who can stand up to the sons of Anak?' But understand that today the Lord your God will cross over ahead of you as a consuming fire; He will devastate and subdue them before you. You will drive them out and destroy them swiftly, as the Lord has told you.* Deuteronomy 9:2,3. They will certainly achieve success in their ongoing battles.

This leads Moshe to warn them not to make any connections between ADONAI's support and Israel's supposed righteousness. Again, his words are very stark and clear - *You are not going to take possession of their land because of your righteousness or your integrity. Instead, the Lord your God will drive out these nations before you because* *of their wickedness, in order to keep the promise He swore to your fathers, Abraham, Isaac, and Jacob. Understand that the L*ORD *your God is not giving you this good land to possess because of your righteousness, for you are a stiff-necked people.* Deuteronomy 9:5,6.

In the remainder of Chapter 9, Moshe recounts Israel's rebellions against ADONAI. Right after they had agreed to follow His life instructions, they rebelled and created a golden calf as their idol. Moshe continued with a list of complaints and agitations, brought on by Israel's stiff-necked approach to ADONAI's authority.

Read Moshe's clear accusation in verse 24 - *You have been rebelling against the L*ORD *ever since I have known you.*

In the final portion of Chapter 9, Moshe shares with his people, his prayers for them. Here is a portion of that prayer, as we read in Deuteronomy 9:26,27 - I prayed to the LORD: *Lord G*OD, *do not annihilate Your people, Your inheritance, whom You redeemed through Your greatness and brought out of Egypt with a strong hand. Remember Your servants Abraham, Isaac, and Jacob. Disregard this people's stubbornness, and their wickedness and sin.*

In Chapter 10, Moshe continues with his recounting of Israel's journey. Here he focused on two major components, a review of the covenant Israel agreed to follow, as they stood before Mt. Sinai, and what ADONAI demanded of His people.

In his review of the covenant, Moshe focused on the process of cutting the two stones upon which ADONAI wrote the Ten Commandments and the creation of the arc of the Covenant, which was placed in the Sanctuary. Verse 5 brings these two aspects together, as Moshe proclaimed, *I went back down the mountain and placed the tablets in the ark I had made. And they have remained there, as the L*ORD *commanded me.*

In verses 10 and 11, Moshe concludes this portion of Chapter 10 by telling Israel of ADONAI's decision not to punish Israel for their disbelief. We read this in verses 10 and 11, *I stayed on the mountain 40 days and 40 nights like the first time. The L*ORD *also listened to me on this occasion; He agreed not to annihilate you. Then the L*ORD *said to me, 'Get up. Continue your journey ahead of the people, so that they may enter and possess the land I swore to give their fathers.*

In the second portion of Chapter 10, Moshe makes very clear the heart of ADONAI's demands of Israel are the heart of Torah, *And now, Israel, what does the L*ORD *your God ask of you except to fear the L*ORD *your God by walking in all His ways, to love*

Him, and to worship the LORD your God with all your heart and all your soul, as we read in verse 12.

Verse 16 brings an important command from ADONAI - *Therefore, circumcise your hearts and don't be stiff-necked any longer.* (Deuteronomy 10:16). This verse will be discussed more fully, below. It is indeed important to understand the connection between being saved and born-again and having our hearts circumcised.

The remainder of the chapter delves more deeply into an explanation of why Israel should obey this command. Here is a portion of what Moshe shared with Israel, *You also must love the foreigner, since you were foreigners in the land of Egypt. You are to fear Yahweh your God and worship Him. Remain faithful to Him and take oaths in His name. He is your praise and He is your God, who has done for you these great and awesome works your eyes have seen. Your fathers went down to Egypt, 70 people in all, and now the LORD your God has made you as numerous as the stars of the sky,* as we read in Deuteronomy 10:19-22.

Chapter 11 begins Moshe's direct teaching to the current generation of Israelites. These are the ones who followed the deceased generation, who frequently rebelled against ADONAI and Moshe and who perished in the wilderness. Notice how Moshe phrases his approach, *You must understand today that it is not your children who experienced or saw the discipline of the LORD your God . . . . Keep every command I am giving you today, so that you may have the strength to cross into and possess the land you are to inherit, and so that you may live long in the land the LORD swore to your fathers to give them and their descendants, a land flowing with milk and honey.* Deuteronomy 11:2,8-9.

The opening sentence of chapter 11 sets the tone for the whole teaching: *Therefore, love the LORD your God and always keep His mandate and His statutes, ordinances, and commands.* Deuteronomy 11:1. Throughout this teaching, Moshe warns his people to continuously focus their attention on keeping ADONAI's teachings in their minds and hearts.

In verses 18-20 of Deuteronomy 11, we read the second half of the traditional *Sh'ma* ceremony. Called the *V'ahavta,* this liturgical piece calls upon Israel to give their entire beings to loving and following ADONAI. Here is a small portion: *Imprint these words of mine on your hearts and minds, bind them as a sign on your hands, and let them be a symbol on your foreheads. Teach them to your children, talking about them when you sit in your house and when you walk along the road, when you lie down and when you get up.* Deuteronomy 11:18,19.

In following verses, Moshe shares more of ADONAI's blessings with Israel: *For if you carefully observe every one of these commands I am giving you to follow -- to love the LORD your God, walk in all His ways, and remain faithful to Him -- the LORD will drive out all these nations before you, and you will drive out nations greater and stronger than you are.* Deuteronomy 11:22,23. Naturally, these blessings are contingent with Israel holding firm to their following ADONAI's commands: *When you possess it and settle in it, be careful to follow all the statutes and ordinances I set before you today.* Deuteronomy 31,32.

DEEPER UNDERSTANDINGS

YOU ARE A HOLY PEOPLE

As we learned earlier, ADONAI chose Israel to be His people, not because of any other factor than He wanted then to teach the world to worship His commands. We find this reference to Israel being ADONAI's chosen people throughout Scripture. For example, in Exodus 19:5, we read: *Now if you will listen to Me and carefully keep My covenant, you will be My own possession out of all the peoples, although all the earth is Mine.* It is important to remember ADONAI YESHUA'S comments in John 14:15, when He proclaimed, *If you love Me, you will keep My commands.* Then in 2 Samuel 7:23, we find - *God came to one nation on earth in order to redeem a people for Himself, to make a name for Himself, and to perform for them great and awesome acts, driving out nations and their gods before Your people You redeemed for Yourself from Egypt.* Our final example comes from Hebrews 8:10, as Rav Sha'ul, the Apostle Paul, is teaching the 1st Century Israelites, *I will put My laws into their minds and write them on their hearts. I will be their God, and they will be My people.* In all, there are more than 20 references to Israel being ADONAI's chosen people throughout Scripture. However the most convincing evidence may be found in Deuteronomy 7:7,8, where Moshe tells Israel, *The LORD was devoted to you and chose you, not because you were more numerous than all peoples, for you were the fewest of all peoples. But because the LORD loved you and kept the oath He swore to your fathers, He brought you out with a strong hand and redeemed you from the place of slavery, from the power of Pharaoh king of Egypt.*

We are living in difficult times. Everywhere around the world, Israel and the Jewish people are being demeaned and cursed. Does this mean ADONAI has dropped Israel as His 'chosen people'? Not at all! Israel will always be Adonai's Chosen People. He does not change; He is consistent in His thinking and in His actions!

MANNA

Manna was introduced to us in Exodus 16 and had the appearance of *coriander seed, was white, and tasted like wafers made with honey.* (Exodus 16:31). Like all good things, when we experience them often, manna became nothing more than something Israel had to scrape from the wilderness ground every morning. ADONAI's providing them with this tasty dish did nothing to stop their grumbling.

DON'T FORGET **ADONAI** YOUR GOD

There is a certain irony in the words Moshe used in this teaching. Yes, ADONAI had warned him of Israel's coming apostasy; the troubles which would befall His people; and, yes, Moshe tried to pass on the dangers facing them, if they turned their backs on their Abba. However, it seems this lesson did not stick and, very shortly into their stay in Cana'an, they started to drift away from Him, engaging in synchronistic practice of worshipping ADONAI and Cana'anite idols[19]. We read of this in Judges 6 to 8.

FACING THE ANAKIM

As you may remember, Israel faced the Anakim when their 12 spies ventured into Cana'an, as recorded in Numbers 13 and 14. They went with ADONAI's protection and support; however, when the spies returned with a less than favourable account of their observations of the giants, the Anakim, and despite the encouragement and faithfulness of Y'hoshua and Kalev the people rebelled against Moshe and ADONAI, threatening to stone both Moshe and Aharon. This was the last straw for ADONAI and He then demanded Israel wander the wilderness for the next 38 years, until that generation died.

Here, then, when Israel is about to face their formidable foe, Moshe wants them to truly understand ADONAI's support, His might, is with them. While Israel will be going into battle with the Anakim, it will be ADONAI who be routing them.

MOSHE'S WARNING

Moshe certainly does know his people. In this section of Chapter 9, Moshe warns them about assuming their righteousness is the reason for ADONAI's support in their battles with the Anakim. Rather, ADONAI has made it quite clear, He is supporting Israel because of the pledge He made to *Avraham* (Abraham), *Yitzchak* (Isaac) and *Ya'akov* (Jacob) in the covenant He <u>unilaterally</u> cut with them. By calling Israel a *'stiff-necked people'*, Moshe is reminding them of their obstinance in refusing to obey ADONAI's commands.

ISRAEL'S REBELLIONS

Some in the biblical commentary[20] world believe Israel was greatly affected by the mixed multitude of non-Jews who joined them in the Exodus from Egypt. As we have learned, the mixed multitude consisted of members of other ethnicities, captured by Egypt and made to be slaves, as well as Egyptians who had been convinced of the

---

[19] Fletcher, E., *Worship of idols in Israel*, https://womeninthebible.net/bible-archaeology/idols_bible/, 2006, accessed 06 January, 2023.

[20] Wisnefsky, Moshe Yaakov, *Mistake of the Mixed Multitude*, Chabad.org, https://www.chabad.org/kabbalah/article_cdo/aid/702396/jewish/Mistake-of-the-Mixed-Multitude.htm, accessed 15 January, 2023.

power of ADONAI. They had a different mind-set than did the Hebrews (Israel) and, perhaps, attempted to guide Israel back to Egypt. Commentators have advanced theories concerning the influence of the mixed multitude upon Israel. For example, Yitzchak Luria[21], a rabbi in the 16th Century, wrote, *[As we have explained elsewhere,] the Mixed Multitude derive from the evil [aspect] of Moses…* Luria contends that allowing the mixed multitude to join in the flight from Egypt was a mistake, based on Moshe's desire to bring them to holiness, through association with Israel. However, as he pointed out, without the thorough teaching Israel had of their Jewish fathers, the mixed multitude was not able to abide by the same rules of faith that guided Israel. Thus, they relied more on their old ways in Egypt which, as we saw at Mt. Sinai, led them to their first bout of idolatry.

During their time in slavery, estimated to be between 86 and 116 years,[22] Israel engaged in syncretic belief. They had been taught to worship and honour ADONAI, the God of their ancestors, Avraham, Yitzchak and Ya'akov, and, when they entered slavery, they were forced to worship the Egyptian gods. Over the years, then, the two forms of worship melded together. Thus, Israel was receptive, when the mixed multitude exerted their influence, during period of perceived strife.

REVIEW OF THE COVENANT

As we read in Exodus 19 and 20, the Covenant was not the Ten Commandments of the Torah, but the agreement Israel made to follow ADONAI's commandments. Let's review that agreement, found in Exodus 19:3-8, *Moses went up the mountain to God, and the LORD called to him from the mountain: This is what you must say to the house of Jacob, and explain to the Israelites: 'You have seen what I did to the Egyptians and how I carried you on eagles' wings and brought you to Me. Now if you will listen to Me and carefully keep My covenant, you will be My own possession out of all the peoples, although all the earth is Mine, and you will be My kingdom of priests and My holy nation.' These are the words that you are to say to the Israelites." After Moses came back, he summoned the elders of the people and set before them all these words that the LORD had commanded him. Then all the people responded together, "We will do all that the LORD has spoken." So, Moses brought the people's words back to the*

---

[21] Luria Y., Op.Cit.

[22] Rosenfeld, D., *Duration of slavery in Egypt*, Aish, https://aish.com/duration-of-slavery-in-egypt/, accessed 16 January, 2023.

LORD *(emphasis mine).* If neither the Ten Commandments nor the Torah were the Covenant, what were they?

As Tzvi Freeman[23] explains, in 'What is Torah', the Torah is a <u>symbol</u> of the Covenant ADONAI made with Israel, as they stood at the base of Mt. Sinai, two months after leaving Egypt. The Ten Commandments, being part of Torah, provide the same symbolic reference.

The covenant has been a source of argument in the believing community for centuries. Many Christians believe that since the 'Old Covenant' has been destroyed, in favour of the 'New Covenant', Torah has been removed from their reading. Do you see an issue with this position?

WHAT DOES ADONAI ASK OF ISRAEL?

There are two complementary foci in response to this question. The first is found in Leviticus 19:18, wherein we find: *Do not take revenge or bear a grudge against members of your community, but love your neighbor as yourself; I am Yahweh.* Rabbi Maralee Gordon, writing in The Heart of the Torah[24], claims, *When a stranger resides with you*

---

[23] Freeman, T., *What is Torah: a comprehensive overview*, Chabad.org, <u>https://www.chabad.org/library/article cdo/aid/1426382/jewish/Torah.htm</u>, accessed 16 January, 2023.

[24] Gordon, M. *The heart of the Torah*, T'ruah, the rabbinic call for human rights, <u>https://truah.org/resources/the-heart-of-the-torah/</u> accessed 16 January 2023.

in your land, you shall not wrong him. The stranger who resides with you shall be to you as one of your citizens; you shall love him as yourself, for you were strangers in the land of Egypt: I the Lord am your God, found in Leviticus 19:33,34, is the true heart of Torah, as it related directly to Israel's release from slavery in Egypt and the celebration of this event through the *Pesach,* Passover, one of the appointed times of ADONAI, annual Seder.

Another group of scholars[25] claims the heart of Torah is the command for us to love ADONAI with all our hearts, minds and resources, as found in Deuteronomy 6:4,5. The Sh'ma command drives the heart of ADONAI's people to maintain a life based on love, giving to others and justice. They claim loving ADONAI is an act of obedience to His commands and is based on love itself, not duty or obligation. What do you think?

SECOND GENERATION ISRAEL

As we read earlier in Deuteronomy, the first generation of Israelites and the Mixed Multitude died, as they wandered through the wilderness. This was as a result of their mistrust of ADONAI and Moshe. Remember, as Moshe recounted, there were ten times his people challenged the decrees made by ADONAI, through Moshe, and for this they were punished. Thus, the entire first generation, with the exception of Kalev and Y'hoshua (Numbers 14:24), was condemned to perish in the wilderness.

The second generation, born in the wilderness, did not participate in either the complaints of their parents nor in their rebellions. The sins of their fathers did not rest on their shoulders. Why would ADONAI allow the second generation of Israelites to escape the punishment for the sins of their fathers, when He clearly stated in Exodus 20 and 34, Numbers 14, Jeremiah 31, Ezekiel 18 and Job 21, just to name a few, that He would visit the sins of the fathers on their sons and daughters? In Exodus 20:5, for example, we read - *punishing the children for the fathers' sin, to the third and fourth generations of those who hate Me.* However, it is important to read the following verse, verse 6: *but showing faithful love to a thousand generations of those who love Me and keep My commands.* In this passage, ADONAI is referring to the sin of idolatry. If the next generation returns to the practice of worshipping ADONAI only, then the consequences for the sins of the fathers will not be laid on the children.

Reading the qualifier in verse 5 indicates to us that ADONAI will visit the sins of the father onto his children, if the father hates Him. What does hating ADONAI mean? When things we consider bad, illness, death of loved ones, financial difficulties, come upon us, we often turn away from ourselves and focus on something or someone

---

[25] Wyse, J.A., Carlson, J. W., Williams, J.T. and Barker, A., eds., <u>Take this word to heart: the Shema in Torah and Gospel</u>, Occasional Papers #23, Institute of Mennonite Studies, Elkhart, Indiana, 2005.

outside ourselves to blame. Often that 'someone' is ADONAI. We have been taught or we have concluded from all the sermons we've

heard about ADONAI's love, that He only brings love to us. Thus, we assume, a loving God would never bring hardship or harm onto the ones He loves. We forget that many of the incidents we face are a direct result of the consequences of our free-will choices. We often ignore the reality that ADONAI seldom intervenes in humans' lives, allowing us the receive the consequences of our actions, or the actions of others on our behalf. For example, following research conducted by the Canadian Cancer Society[26], there are only two causes of cancer that are not within our control: age and heredity. Many others, such as smoking, lack of protection from the sun, obesity, unhealthy diet, lack of physical activity, alcohol, unhealthy lifestyle, etc., are within our control, either as individuals or as a society.

ADONAI is our perfect Father and He knows when we need a challenge to push us to explore His love for us more closely or to examine our lives, so as to come closer to the children He wants us to be. One thing we often forget: ADONAI's understanding of time is not our sense of time. We cannot impose our desires and needs on Him and expect He will answer us positively when we want Him to do so.

Thus, ADONAI must have believed the second generation of Israelites did not share many of their fathers' hatred for ADONAI and did not or were not going to abandon His path. They appeared to be closer to ADONAI than did their fathers and mothers.

In verses 10 and 11 of Chapter 10, we are also given a clue to ADONAI's decision to allow the second generation of Israelites to live. Here we find His covenant with their ancestors, Avraham, Yitzchak and Ya'akov, was considered very seriously and that covenant could not be fulfilled if Israel no longer existed.

LAND OF MILK AND HONEY

In Deuteronomy 8:8,9 we find the following verse - *a land of wheat, barley, vines, figs, and pomegranates; a land of olive oil and honey; a land where you will eat food without shortage, where you will lack nothing.* ADONAI has promised Israel bountiful returns, when they occupy the Promised Land; these returns are based on their love and commitment to Him and Him alone. ADONAI has provided for Israel in both the Spring and the Fall Feasts. The Spring Feasts (Pesach-Passover; and Shavu'ot/Pentecost) lead us to ADONAI YESHUA and His first appearance, while

---

[26] Canadian Cancer Society, *What causes cancer?* https://cancer.ca/en/cancer-information/what-is-cancer/what-causes-cancer, accessed 01 February, 2023.

the Fall Feasts (Yom Teruah – Day of Trumpets, Yom Kippur – Day of Atonement, and Sukkot - Tabernacling) are signals to His return, at the end of days.

CIRCUMCISE YOUR HEARTS

We read this command in Deuteronomy 10:16. This is also found in Jeremiah 4, as we read, *Break up the unplowed ground; do not sow among the thorns. Circumcise yourselves to the LORD; remove the foreskin of your hearts, men of Judah and residents of Jerusalem. Otherwise, My wrath will break out like fire and burn with no one to extinguish it because of your evil deeds.* Like many of ADONAI'S pronouncements, this one too takes on an agricultural façade. Our Lord is urging His people to break their hard hearts and stop being lured by the adversary to plant their lives in his hard ground. By commanding them to *remove the foreskin of your hearts,* ADONAI is ordering them to break out of the hardness that surrounds their minds and actions and become more humble before ADONAI.

Rav Sha'ul, the Apostle Paul, mentions this in Romans 2:29, when he writes - *circumcision is of the heart—by the Spirit, not the letter.*

Many believers think, from reading only the 'New Testament', the Apostolic Scriptures, circumcision of the heart could only occur during the time of ADONAI YESHUA'S time on earth and afterward. As we see, this concept originated in the Hebrew Scriptures, the 'Old Testament'

The V'ahavta

In Deuteronomy 6:5, we read a portion of the V'ahavta, recited during the Sh'ma. The V'ahavta, which means – And you shall love, focuses on what must be our behaviour at all times. As we read it carefully, we may see it represents the *Aséret ha-D'Varim*, the Ten Commandments. Having been added to the Sh'ma hundreds of years ago, this now forms the most foundational commandment in Torah. The Sh'ma is recited every morning, when waking, and every evening, when retiring. The V'ahavta is recited usually during morning prayers. Below is the full contents of V'ahavta:

You shall love ADONAI your God with all your heart,
with all your soul, and with all your might.
Take to heart these instructions with which I charge you this day.
Impress them upon your children.
Recite them when you stay at home and when you are away,
when you lie down and when you get up.
Bind them as a sign on your hand and let them serve as a symbol on your forehead;
inscribe them on the doorposts of your house and on your gates.

This concludes the explanation of our third weekly reading.

May the God of Abraham, Isaac and Jacob bless you fully and richly.

Parashah Re-eh (See)

Deuteronomy 11:26 –16:17

This, our fourth weekly reading, focuses on the bulk of the commandments found in HaSefer D'Varim, the Book of Deuteronomy. Moshe warns his people that their choice to accept or reject ADONAI's commands amounts to a choice between receiving blessings or curses.

Please read the passage focused on here before you engage the text.

PARASHAH RE-EH (SEE, BEHOLD)

DEUTERONOMY 11:26 –16:17

Look, today I set before you a blessing and a curse: there will be a blessing, if you obey the commands of the LORD your God I am giving you today, and a curse, if you do not obey the commands of the LORD your God and you turn aside from the path I command you today by following other gods you have not known.

Deuteronomy 11:26-28

The entirety of this week's Torah reading, Deuteronomy 11:26 to 16:17, focuses on ADONAI's regulations and teachings to His children, Israel. We begin with Moshe issuing His commands to place the blessings on Mount Gerizim and the curses on Mount Ebal. These mountains, both west of the Yarden River near Schechem, stand opposite each other. Chapter 11 ends with the cautionary words: *When you possess it and settle in it, be careful to follow all the statutes and ordinances I set before you today.* Deuteronomy 11:31,32.

The first set of instructions, found in this reading, focus on how Israel was to deal with the spiritual places of the Cana'anites. Here is a portion of this instruction: *Destroy completely all the places where the nations that you are driving out worship their gods—on the high mountains, on the hills, and under every green tree. Tear down their altars, smash their sacred pillars, burn up their Asherah poles, cut down the carved images of their gods, and wipe out their names from every place.* Deuteronomy 12:2,3.

When this task was completed, Moses shared with his people that ADONAI would tell them,through Yahoshua, Joshua, where they should place His Tabernacle for their future worship. Listen to a portion of this command – *When you cross the Jordan and live in the land the LORD your God is giving you to inherit, and He gives you rest from all the enemies around you and you live in security, then Yahweh your God will choose the place to have His name dwell. Bring there everything I command you: your burnt offerings, sacrifices, offerings of the tenth, personal contributions, and all your choice offerings you vow to the LORD.* Deuteronomy 12:10,11.

The next set of instructions focus on the animals that Israel was to eat. As we read in verses 16 and 17 of Deuteronomy 12, any animal within the city gates of Israel, may be slaughtered and eaten. The designation of 'any animal' is discussed below. Verse 22 is clear about who may eat the meat - *Indeed, you may eat it as the gazelle and deer are eaten; both the clean and the unclean may eat it.*

However, none of the blood of the animal was to be eaten, as we read in verses 23 and 24: *But don't eat the blood, since the blood is the life, and you must not eat the life with the meat. Do not eat blood; pour it on the ground like water.* The blessing for not eating blood is quite clear, as we read in verse 25 - *Do not eat it, so that you and your children after you will prosper, because you will be doing what is right in the LORD's sight.* Incidentally, the curse is also clear.

Offerings, such as the tenth of the grain, new wine and oil, and the other fellowship offerings, were to be taken to the designated location ADONAI was to indicate once Israel entered the new land. Deuteronomy 14:23. These gifts were to be eaten by the family once they had been offered to ADONAI. Finally, in this section of chapter12, Israel is cautioned to look after the Levites within their villages, as they had no inheritance of the land. ADONAI was their inheritance.

In Chapter 13, we find Moshe teaching Israel ways in which they are to deal with false prophets and teachers. In verses 1 to 3, Moshe says: *If a prophet or someone who has dreams arises among you and proclaims a sign or wonder to you, and that sign or wonder he has promised you comes about, but he says, 'Let us follow other gods,' which you have not known, 'and let us worship them,' do not listen to that prophet's words or to that dreamer. For the LORD your God is testing you to know whether you love the LORD your God with all your heart and all your soul.* The punishment for spreading false teachings is death, as mentioned in verse 5.

ADONAI instructed Israel to always be on the watch for anyone who enticed them to engage in idolatry, as we read in verses 6 to 18 of Chapter 13. Let's read verses 6 to 11: *"If your brother, the son of your mother, or your son or daughter, or the wife you embrace, or your closest friend secretly entices you, saying, 'Let us go and worship other gods'—which neither you nor your fathers have known, any of the gods of the peoples around you, near you or far from you, from one end of the earth to the other— you must not yield to him or listen to him. Show him no pity, and do not spare him or shield him. Instead, you must kill him. Your hand is to be the first against him to put him to death, and then the hands of all the people. Stone him to death for trying to turn you away from the Lord your God who brought you out of the land of Egypt, out of the place of slavery. All Israel will hear and be afraid, and they will no longer do anything evil like this among you."*

Verses 12 to 15 solidify ADONAI's teaching, through Moshe, of the dangers of following false prophets and teachers: *If you hear it said about one of your cities the Lord your God is giving you to live in, that wicked men have sprung up among you, led the inhabitants of their city astray, and said, 'Let us go and worship other gods,' which you have not known, If the report turns out to be true that this detestable thing has happened among you, you must strike down the inhabitants of that city with the sword. Completely destroy everyone in it as well as its livestock with the sword.* This final command given by ADONAI, through Moshe, in Chapter 13, focuses on dealing with a community being infiltrated by corrupt men who are bent on leading Israel astray. When these men are discovered, they and all those following them are to be exterminated and all their possessions burned in the town square.

One of the practices of the ancient world focused on dealing with the dead. ADONAI had instructed Moshe on one of these – honouring the dead by self-mutilation. In Chapter 14:1,2, Moshe instructs his people to avoid engaging in these practices, confirming with them, *The Lord has chosen you to be His own possession out of all the peoples on the face of the earth.* Deuteronomy 14:2

As we have read in Leviticus 11, ADONAI clearly indicated the animals Israel was to eat. This ruling is further emphasized in Deuteronomy 14:3-21. Here is a brief statement of this ruling: *You may eat any animal that has hooves divided in two and chews the cud. . . . You may eat everything from the water that has fins and scales. . . . You may eat every clean bird. . . .* Deuteronomy 14:6,9,19. All these animals became known as food for Israel.

As a final statement in this teaching, Moshe informed Israel they were not to eat from the carcass of any animal that had died naturally, which had not been bled properly. However, as we read in verse 21, *you may give it to a temporary resident living within your gates, and he may eat it, or you may sell it to a foreigner.* Once more, this teaching ends with the very clear phrase, *For you are a holy people belonging to the Lord your God.* Deuteronomy 14:21.

The final command in this teaching is *You must not boil a young goat in its mother's milk.* Deuteronomy 14:21. This teaching has created some consternation among Rabbinic and Messianic Jews, which is discussed below.

Chapter 15 leads us to an understanding of the cancellation of debts, during the *Shemitah,* the seventh year after reaching the promised land. We read of this commandment from Moshe in verses 1 to 3. Let's read a small portion of the passage: *At the end of every seven years you must cancel debts.* Deuteronomy 15:1. Moshe concludes this portion with the words, *When the LORD your God blesses you as He has promised you, you will lend to many nations but not borrow; you will rule over many nations, but they will not rule over you.* Deuteronomy 15:6.

We continue with the command to be generous with the poor, who wait by the town gate to receive the generosity of passers-by. Listen to Moshe's command to his people - *Give to him, and don't have a stingy heart when you give, and because of this the LORD your God will bless you in all your work and in everything you do.* Deuteronomy 15:10. However, if Israelites are stingy towards the poor, Moshe has a harsh word for them: (if) *you are stingy toward your poor brother and give him nothing. He will cry out to the LORD against you, and you will be guilty.* Deuteronomy 15:9.

The Shemitah year is very important to all of mankind, as we read in the following verses, of Chapter 15. During this period of time all the slaves the Israelites had were to be released and provided with the provisions to continue with their free lives. There were some conditions on their release, however. If they obtained wives and children while in slavery these were to remain with the master, as we read in Exodus 21:4. However, as we read in verses 16 and 17 of Deuteronomy 15, if they wished to stay with their slavery families, under their masters' care, they were to allow their masters to hammer an awl into their right ear lobes. Thus, they were their masters' slaves for life. Moshe's comment, recorded in verse 18, tells us how important this releasing of slaves was for Israel - *Do not regard it as a hardship when you set him free, because he worked for you six years -- worth twice the wages of a hired hand. Then the LORD your God will bless you in everything you do.*

The final issue of Chapter 15 is that of the first-born male of the livestock. When the first-born male of cattle, sheep and goats arrived, they were to be set-aside for ADONAI. These were to be used as offerings and sacrifices. As we read in the Book of Judges 21, they were to be taken to Shilo, and later Jerusalem, to be slaughtered and then eaten in the Presence of ADONAI. We read this in verses 19 and 20: *All the firstborn males in your herd of cattle and in your flock, you are to set aside for ADONAI your God; you are not to do any work with a firstborn from your herd or shear a firstborn sheep. Each year you and your household are to eat it in the presence of ADONAI your God in the place which ADONAI will choose.*

If any of the first born had a defect, such as a broken limb or deformed genitalia, they could be eaten by the family on their own property, rather than used as sacrifices of offerings. Once again, Moshe instructed his people not to eat the blood, but to pour it onto the ground. We read of these provisions in verses 21 to 23: *But if there is a defect in the animal, if it is lame or blind or has any serious defect, you must not sacrifice it to the LORD your God. Eat it within your gates; both the unclean person and the clean may eat it, as though it were a gazelle or deer. But you must not eat its blood; pour it on the ground like water.*

Most of Chapter 16 focuses on the Spring Feasts, Pesach (Passover), Hag HaMatzot, (the Feast of Unleavened Bread),the *Omer,* and *Shavu'ot* (Pentecost). Pesach begins on Aviv 14. Each family is to sacrifice an animal from their herd or flock, at the place ADONAI has commanded for all sacrifices. Once the portions of the animal are sacrificed, the family takes the rest back to their home for eating. We see this command in verse 2 - *Sacrifice to Yahweh your God a Passover animal from the herd or flock in the place where the LORD chooses to have His name dwell.* Moshe then teaches his people to eat only unleavened bread, *matzah,* for the seven days of the festival. Here is the verse that provides the rationale for this practice: *For seven days you are to eat unleavened bread with it, the bread of hardship—because you left the land of Egypt in a hurry—so that you may remember for the rest of your life the day you left the land of Egypt.* Deuteronomy 16:3.

Verses 9 to 12 of Chapter 16 share with us the counting of the omer and the Festival of Shavu'ot. Here is a segment of that commandment: *You are to count seven weeks; you are to begin counting seven weeks from the time you first put your sickle to the standing grain. You are to celebrate the Festival of Weeks to the LORD your God with a freewill offering that you give in proportion to how the LORD your God has blessed you.* Deuteronomy 16:9,10. The grain referenced in this verse is wheat, used for making bread and pastries.

Shavu'ot is a harvest festival when the wheat crop is gathered. Wheat is the predominate grain used in making matzah. As believers know, Christians call this holy day Pentecost, from the Greek for 50th. This was the giving of the Blessed Holy Spirit of the Living God to the disciples.

All Israel was to provide volunteer offerings in accordance with the size of their respective harvest; the greater the harvest, the larger the offering and, conversely, the smaller the harvest the smaller the offering. Read this in verse 10: *You are to observe the festival of Shavu'ot [weeks] for ADONAI your God with a voluntary offering, which you are to give in accordance with the degree to which ADONAI your God has prospered you.* In this way, Israel would continuously thank their provider for His generosity.

Verse 12 is significant, in that Moshe reminds his people that their freedom comes entirely from ADONAI: *Remember that you were a slave in Egypt; then you will keep and obey these laws.* In the previous verse, verse 11, Moshe again informs Israel that the Tabernacle will be placed in a secure location, where everyone will attend and rejoice, at specific times.

Verse 13 reiterates the directive to keep the Festival of Sukkot, Tabernacles or Booths, for seven days, from 15 Tishrei to 21 Tishrei, sometime in late September, early October on the Gregorian calendar. This festival recognizes the fruit harvest and gives ADONAI the glory for producing a bountiful harvest. This is time of rejoicing and gathering together in community.

This completes the reading for this week.

DEEPER UNDERSTANDINGS

MOUNT GERIZIM AND MOUNT EBAL

These two mountains are situated in relation to each other in such a way that when anything is spoken on either mount, it may be heard on the other. This was the perfect site, then, for ADONAI's blessings and curses to be read to Israel. As we will read later, in Deuteronomy 27, the tribes of Reuben, Gad, Asher, Zebulun, Dan, and Naphtali were to stand on Mount Ebal and the tribes of Simeon, Levi, Judah, Issachar, Joseph, and Benjamin were to stand on Mount Gerizim.

DESTROYING THE HIGH PLACES OF CANA'AN

ADONAI was Israel's Ruler, their Suzerain. As such, it was His privilege to remove all the sites of worship established in the land by the Cana'anites. Removing these sites would remove added temptation from Israel to shift their worship from Him to the idols and foreign gods of this land. This teaching reminded Israel that they were still under the Covenant ADONAI cut with Avraham, Yitzchak and Ya'akov.

How do we apply this statement today? If you need a suggestion that syncretism is creeping into Christianity today, look not further than the festivals that almost all Christians, and non-Christians celebrate, Christmas and Easter, to name two. Do we know the exact date of Messiah's birth? Unfortunately, no; there are clues we are given in Scripture but even then, these do not lead us to a specific date. As has been written elsewhere, December 25 was not the date of His birth. This date was reserved for the birthdate of the 'unconquerable sun', one of the many deities in the Roman pantheon. Pope Julius 1, in his early days, fixed that date to draw pagans to celebrate YESHUA's birth.

Easter, the date celebrating the resurrection of ADONAI YESHUA, was fixed by the Roman Emperor Constatine in 325 CE, as a way of moving Christians away from celebrating the Festivals of ADONAI.

However, what dates of festivals did members of the early church celebrate? These were the Feasts of ADONAI, Feasts of the LORD. We begin with *Pesach*, Passover, held on the 14th of Aviv, sometime in April. This is a one-day festival followed by the seven day Feast of Unleavened Bread, or Matza. The second day of the Feast of Matza is *Bikkurim*, First Fruits. Bikkurim was the day set aside for the harvesting of barley, the first grain to mature. This is the day ADONAI YESHUA resurrected, after having lain in His tomb for 3 days and nights. He was the First Fruit of the resurrection. Then we have Shavu'ot or Pentecost. This was also a harvest day, this time for wheat. As most of us know, this was the date that the Holy Spirit came to the Apostles and Disciples, gave them the power of speaking in tongues and allowed them to draw 3,000 Jews to believe in ADONAI YESHUA.

The Fall Feasts, consist of *Yom Teruah*, the Day of Trumpets, *Yom Kippur*, the Day of Atonement, and *Sukkot*, the Day of Gathering/Tabernacling. Yom Teruah is the projected season when ADONAI YESHUA will return and occupy His earthly throne as Ruler of His world. Yom Kippur prophesises His Day of Judgment, when all sinners will be judged, to determine their worthiness for either heaven or hell. Finally, Sukkot is the Day of Tabernacles, when ADONAI YESHUA will walk about His earth once more. Many Messianic believers hold this season as the time of His birth, based on biblical clues.

How do we know believers will be judged by ADONAI YESHUA, upon His return? Rav Sha'ul makes this abundantly clear in 2 Corinthians 5:10, when he writes: "for we must all appear before the Messiah's court of judgment, where everyone will receive the good or bad consequences of what he did while he was in the body." However, this does not mean believers will be condemned. Rather, in Romans 8:1 we read – "there is no longer any condemnation awaiting those who are in union with the MESSIAH YESHUA."

Will we ever return to ADONAI's Feasts and abandon those of the idolaters? I don't believe this will happen until ADONAI YESHUA'S return.

CENTRAL LOCATION FOR WORSHIP

Many commentators believe the central location for worship was Jerusalem. One of the many was Rabbi Yishmael,[27] who, in his Midrashic collection, believed that although Jerusalem was not settled by Israel until the time of King David, this was the site

---

[27] Rabbi Yishmael ben Elisha Nachmani, also known as Rabi Yishmael, lived in the period of the late 1st and early 2nd centuries, lived in Kfar Aziz, south of Hebron. He established many of the principles of a logical method by which laws may be deduced from laws and important decisions founded on the plain phraseology of the Scriptures. https://en.wikipedia.org/wiki/Rabbi_Ishmael, accessed 26 February, 2023.

God meant for His Temple to be built. Others, such as the authors of the Samaritan Pentateuch,[28] believe the site of the central place for worship was at Mount Gerizim, located within Samaritan territory.

The Tabernacle was eventually located in Shilo, as we read in the Book of Joshua (Joshua 18:31). It stayed there until Solomon completed ADONAI's Temple, about 966 BCE (before the Common Era).

ANY ANIMAL

ADONAI had clearly outlined to Moshe the animals that could be taken as food. As we recall from Leviticus 11:3, ADONAI told Moshe - *You may eat any animal with divided hooves and that chews the cud.* Animals that did not have a divided hoof or/ and that did not chew its cud could not be eaten.

When the Israelites were wandering through the wilderness, any animal to be slaughtered was to be taken to the Sanctuary, where it would be properly killed, according to ADONAI's stipulations, and then eaten by the family. Each family was sufficiently close to the Tabernacle that this was relatively easy to do. However, once they settled in their new land, this was much more difficult, as the people were scattered throughout the land. There was too great a distance to take the evening animal to the Tabernacle for slaughter. Thus, ADONAI told Moshe that the people could slaughter any of the animals outlined in Leviticus 11:3, they had within the community.

So, the question arises why would ADONAI forbid people to eat any animal, shellfish and some birds? The answer is quite complex and I will attempt to narrow it down a little. There are some health reasons for not eating pork.[29] [30] The answer to this question provided by Torah is, this is the will of ADONAI. Pork was eaten by Israel's neighbours and, as such, was forbidden for Israel.

---

[28] The Samaritans lived in the northern portion of Israel, once inhabited by Israel, while Judah lived in further south. It is believed they were formed from the union of Israelites left after the conquest of Israel by the Persians and Persian soldiers sent to populate the region. Their Torah, or Pentateuch, was the only group of Scriptures authorized to be considered written by ADONAI. The scribes of the Samaritan Pentateuch are long forgotten.

[29] Juber, M., *Is pork bad for you?* MedicineNet, https://www.medicinenet.com/is_pork_bad_for_you_and_is_it_worse_than_beef/article.htm, accessed 30 July, 2024.

[30] Jones, E., *Did Jesus eat pork?* Church of God, Did Jesus Eat Pork? (lifehopeandtruth.com), Accessed 30 July, 2024.

Prohibition on eating Blood

As we learned in Genesis 9:4 and Leviticus 17:13,14, no one should eat meat that contains blood. Let's examine these verses: Genesis 9:4 - *However, you must not eat meat with its lifeblood in it.* This is the first prohibition concerning eating blood. However, there is no explanation for the prohibition. To find this we go to Leviticus 17:13,14, wherein we read - *Any Israelite or foreigner living among them, who hunts down a wild animal or bird that may be eaten must drain its blood and cover it with dirt. Since the life of every creature is its blood, I have told the Israelites: You must not eat the blood of any creature, because the life of every creature is its blood; whoever eats it must be cut off.* In these verses we are told life exists within blood. Thus, if any animal is killed and its blood is not drained, anyone who eats that meat will be cut-off from his/her people. Is there anything in these verses to warn us about drinking blood or eating blood products? We know, from both the Hebrew and the Apostolic Scriptures, blood is needed for atonement (Leviticus 17:11 and Hebrews 9:13,14).

There is an additional issue with regards blood. In Leviticus 19:26, 1 Samuel 14:342,33 and Ezekiel 33:25, the Hebrew, *lo' to' khelu 'al ha-dam,* has been translated as "do not eat over the blood."[31] There are two predominate interpretations of the word 'al'. The first is interpreted as 'with'. This interpretation prohibits the eating of blood, as food. However, this interpretation forbids the spilling of the blood of sacrificed animals on the ground, according with the Deuteronomic Code (Deuteronomy 12:20-25). The Code does allow the spilling of the blood of unclean animals or animals that have been hunted for food (Deuteronomy 12:15). Any animal that has been slaughtered for sacrifice or offering, its blood is to be sprinkled on the altar, the priests or the people, depending on the occasion.

Today blood is considered a raw substance[32] and may contain many harmful bacteria and pathogens that can cause problems if eaten by human beings. If you drink or raw blood, be aware that you may be creating a risk for yourself and others.

Designated location for Worship

When ADONAI required Israel to locate the Tabernacle and, later, the Temple, in a central location, He had a purpose in mind. He knew if He allowed people to prepare sacrifices near their homes, they would soon deviate from His ordinances and shift

---

[31] Milgrom, J., *Blood: Meat,* Jewish Virtual Library, Blood (jewishvirtuallibrary.org), accessed 24 June, 2024.
[32] Clark, C., *Drinking blood: Is it safe?* Healthline, https://www.healthline.com/health/drinking-blood, accessed 30 July, 2027.

towards idolatry. To avoid this, ADONAI mandated a central location for both the Tabernacle and the Temple.

The Tabernacle was housed at Shiloh, a central location for all tribes to bring their sacrifices and offerings. This was the site located following Israel's conquest of the Cana'anite tribes. Following King David's conquest of Jebus, from the Jebusites, in 1,000 BCE, the city was renamed *Yerushalayim,* Jerusalem, and became the capital of Israel. Later, in 957 BCE, Solomon, David's son, built the first Temple in Yerushalayim. In 2 Chronicles 5, we are told that all the items housed in the Tabernacle were moved to the Temple: *All the elders of Israel came, and the Levites picked up the ark. They brought up the ark, the tent of meeting, and the holy utensils that were in the tent. The priests and the Levites brought them up.* 2 Chronicles 5:4,5.

ADONAI WAS THE LEVITES' INHERITANCE

In Deuteronomy 18, we are informed that the Levites would have no share in Israel's inheritance of land. Rather, they would live among the other tribes, once they reached the promised land: *The Levitical priests, the whole tribe of Levi, will have no portion or inheritance with Israel. They will eat the LORD's fire offerings; that is their inheritance. Although Levi has no inheritance among his brothers, the LORD is his inheritance, as He promised him.* Deuteronomy 18:1,2. We first learned of this decree in Numbers 18:23,24 - *The Levites will not receive an inheritance among the Israelites; this is a permanent statute throughout your generations. For I have given them the tenth that the Israelites present to the LORD as a contribution for their inheritance. That is why I told them that they would not receive an inheritance among the Israelites."* Although the Levites had no share in the inherited land holdings of the other tribes, they could own houses within the cities of refuge and could own land that belonged within the sphere of the cities[33]. However, there are two other reasons for the Levites being set apart from the rest of Israel. First, Levi, the son of Ya'akov, joined Simeon in the massacre of the men of Shechem, as we read in Genesis 25, following the abduction and rape of their sister, Dinah, by Shechem, the prince of the region. Thus, Ya'akov ordered both his sons be removed as tribes from Israel. As we learned, Simeon was assimilated into the other tribes of Israel, as Ya'akov prophesized in Genesis 49. This did not mean that Simeon ceased to exist as a tribe, as we read in Joshua 19:1: *The second lot came out for Simeon, for the tribe of his descendants by*

---

[33] Goeman, P., *Levites, the Land, and Acts 4:36-37*, The Bible Sojourner, Levites, the Land, and Acts 4:36-37 – PeterGoeman.com, accessed 24 June, 2024.

their clans, but their inheritance was within the portion of Judah's descendants, and 1 Chronicles 15:9 - *Then he gathered all Judah and Benjamin, as well as those from the tribes of Ephraim, Manasseh, and Simeon who had settled among them, for they had defected to him from Israel in great numbers when they saw that Yahweh his God was with him.*

During the Israelite rebellion against ADONAI, found in Exodus 32 and known as the golden calf, the men of the Levite clan stood with Moshe as He dealt with the rebels. Thus, the Tribe of Levi was set aside by ADONAI to serve as His priests, as we read in Numbers 8:16-18.

FALSE PROPHETS AND TEACHERS

It appears the problem of false prophets and teachers is not relegated to our generation. ADONAI realized that even the Israelites would encounter those who would promote themselves as prophets and teachers of ADONAI's Word for their own purposes. Even if their prophecies and teachings proved correct, they should be punished, if they proceeded to lead Israel astray by promoting believe in other deities and other paths. Indeed, in the ensuing generations, when they were ensconced in Israel, they were met with false teachings of other deities that led them to house idols within their homes. We know this, when we read in Judges 6:7-10 - *When the Israelites cried out to Him because of Midian, the LORD sent a prophet to them. He said to them, "This is what the LORD God of Israel says: 'I brought you out of Egypt and out of the place of slavery. I delivered you from the power of Egypt and the power of all who oppressed you. I drove them out before you and gave you their land. I said to you: I am Yahweh your God. Do not fear the gods of the Amorites whose land you live in. But you did not obey Me.'"*When Israel cried out to ADONAI, He sent them a deliverer, Gideon.

Even today we are faced with false teachers and prophets who seem to easily convince believers to support them and follow their teachings. The internet is filled with these names, from well-respected researchers. I urge you to seek these out.

Also, there are false doctrines and creeds being presented that I can share with you. A few of these include:

Worshipping Mary as God;
ADONAI YESHUA, the LORD JESUS, is not God;
Messiah's blood does not atone for our sins; and
Speaking in tongues that are not known languages.

Beloved, please be aware of the dangers of listening to and following false teachers. Stay grounded in the Word of Adonai, our solid Anchor! If you are interested, I suggest you look at <u>(13) 10 Characteristics of False Teachers | LinkedIn</u>; this will provide you with several ways of determining if a prophet or teacher is spreading false doctrine.

BOILING MEAT

The command, *You must not boil a young goat in its mother's milk,* (Deuteronomy 14:21) has created much consternation amongst Rabbinic and Messianic Jews, and with much speculation. From this one statement, Orthodox Jewish rabbis have brought forth the ruling that, literally, meat and milk products are not to be mixed. This is contained in a series of fence-laws, designed to safe guard the possibility of violating the command given in Deuteronomy 14. As a result, in the home, rabbis contend, one must have two refrigerators, two sinks, two sets of dishes and two sets of pots, pans and utensils for cooking and eating – one for meat and one for milk products. As well, there is a prohibition of serving milk at the same table as meat. However, there are health considerations to be reflected upon.

Medical researchers have long known that drinking milk while eating meat can cause some reactions, moderate to severe.

Obviously, the implementation of this and other fence-laws raises the question of cost. With young observant Jews starting out in life required to have two of everything in their kitchen, this would be quite expensive and, without the support of others, mainly parents and family, would be impossible to implement.

Clearly, this has created a major debate amongst Messianic Jews. There are those who follow the command and there are those who do not follow. However, theology has also entered this discussion[34].

Often raised in this discussion are ADONAI YESHUA'S own words, quoted in Mark 7:15 and explained more fully in verse 19: *Nothing that goes into a person from outside can defile him, but the things that come out of a person are what defile him . . . . For it doesn't go into his heart but into the stomach and is eliminated." (As a result, He made all foods clean.)*. And herein lies the problem.

In the final statement, contained in parentheses, it appears that ADONAI YESHUA is stating that all foods are clean, meaning, even the eating of pork and shellfish, amongst others, is allowed. However, ADONAI YESHUA would never

---

[34] For deeper discussions of this command, please read and listen to: <u>Does God's Law Prohibit Cheeseburgers?</u> <u>(Deuteronomy 14:21) - 119 Ministries (youtube.com)</u>, from 119 Ministries; <u>A Kid in Its Mother's Milk – Hebrew In Israel</u>, from Hebrew in Israel and <u>Do not boil a young goat in its mother's milk: another possibility. - Seeking Scripture</u>, from Seeking Scripture.

violate His own ordinances. When He and His followers, Israeli Jews, spoke of food, they always focused on the definitions of food outlined in Torah. Thus, the phrase, *He made all foods clean*, only refers to those animals considered clean and processed properly. Notice, too, that the phrase is enclosed in parentheses, indicating it was added by others and is not contained in the original manuscripts of Mark's writings. The context of YESHUA'S teaching focuses on the importance of inner purity, the nature of sin and the significance of one's heart.

However, for believers, this insertion creates an immense problem. If ADONAI YESHUA cancelled a command given by His Father, Almighty GOD, then He could not be the Messiah. If only one piece of Torah is removed, the totality of Torah is abrogated. The result of this is staggering – salvation is a lie.

THE SH'MITTAH

In Exodus 23:10, we are introduced to the *Sh'mittah*, the seventh year of planting and harvesting. Just as ADONAI wanted rest for His people, on the seventh day, Shabbat, He also wanted rest for the land. Here in Deuteronomy 15, we read of the requirement for all Israel to release the debts they hold against their brother Israelites. This means, if a fellow Israelite owes a debt and has indentured himself or herself as payment, that person is to be released, to return to his own land, with the debt cancelled.

ATTENTION TO THE POOR

Moshe warned his people there would always be poor among them; as such, they were required to pay attention to them, to show compassion to them and be generous in helping them out of their misery. In this way, Moshe is telling his people they have a responsibility to ensure all peoples are to be treated equitably.

RELEASING SLAVES

Our Abba is a generous and loving God. Although He does allow slavery, for those who are in severe financial difficulty and become bonded slaves, He provides a way they can regain their freedom. The Sh'mittah is held every 7 years. At the 7th year, counted from the time Israel entered the land of Israel, every slave owner was to allow his slaves to leave, with sufficient resources to start their lives over. As we read in Chapter 15, these resources may include money as well as equipment. However, if the male slave married while in slavery, his wife and any children were to remain with the master, as has been earlier explained. As outlines earlier, a female slave receives the same treatment as male slaves. If a female slave marries, she may be freed during the Sh'mittah year, but her husband and any children must remain with the master. As with the male slave, if the female slave wishes to remain with her family, she too will have her ear pierced by an awl.

There was some controversy regarding this ruling. According to Leviticus 25, slaves, who were Israelites, were considered to be hired hands and were to be treated as such (for example, see Israel Knohl [35]). All Israel was considered to be slaves of ADONAI and He was their only Master.

Another interpretation of the freeing of Hebrew slaves, focused on the Sh'mittah year only. As we read in Jeremiah 34, when King Zedekiah ordered slaves to be released, during the Sh'mittah, in 590 (approx.) BCE, slave owners did so and then, at the end of the Sh'mittah, brought them back into slavery, when their labour was again needed.

FIRST-BORN MALE ANIMALS

The Tabernacle was established and situated in Shilo, when Israel entered the land; all sacrifices and offerings were to be made before ADONAI on the altar. These sacrifices and offerings were of the first-born males of cattle, sheep and goats. Torah was very clear about this. Any sacrifices performed at any other location was in violation of Torah. When the tribes of Israel, as opposed to the tribes of Judah, relocated in the territory of Dan, prior to the end of Solomon's reign, in 870-750 BCE, they built their altar of convenience, allowing them not to travel to Jerusalem. This was mentioned in Judges 18 and described in 2 Kings 17. As a result of their apostasy, ADONAI permitted the Assyrians to capture Israel and relocate them to their empire, in 732 BCE.

The male animals used in the sacrifices and offerings had to be pure; that means there was no defect what-so-ever. Such defects include, being lame, blind, having a skin disease, having a missing or deformed testicle. Offering an animal with any of these defects would be considered an insult to ADONAI.

FESTIVAL OF PASSOVER

Interestingly, the Festival of Pesach, Passover, is only a one-day festival, beginning on the 14th of *Aviv* at sundown, the first month of the year. For an additional seven

---

[35] Knohl, I., Shabbat, shemitah and slavery, Shalom Hartman, 2009. https://www.hartman.org.il/shabbat-shmitta-and-slavery-human-freedom-and-the-yoke-of-heaven/, accessed 06 April, 2023.

days, the celebration is the *Hag HaMatzot*, Feast of Matzah, unleavened bread. This is bread that is baked without any leavening agents, yeast, baking powder, etc. Below you will find a picture of matzah.

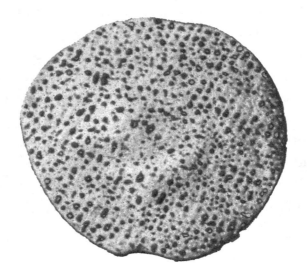

It may be difficult to see the holes punched into this piece, however, you can see the stripes along the face of the piece. Although these refer to the baking process, to ensure no natural leavening can occur, the Scriptural connection is found in Isaiah 53:4,5. Let's read that portion now: *Yet He Himself bore our sicknesses, and He carried our pains; but we in turn regarded Him stricken, struck down by God, and afflicted. But He was pierced because of our transgressions, crushed because of our iniquities; punishment for our peace was on Him, and we are healed by His wounds.* Rabbis are discouraged from reading Isaiah 53 to their community, as the rabbinate recognizes this chapter refers specifically to ADONAI YESHUA, the LORD JESUS.

THE OMER

Israel was commanded by ADONAI, recorded in Leviticus 23, to count the days from the evening of Aviv 16, the second day of the Festival of Unleavened Bread, to the 5th of *Sivan*, a total of 49 days. The next day, Sivan 6, is Shavu'ot, the Feast of Weeks. This day has two markers: The first is the immediate, the day of the gathering of the wheat harvest; the second is a commemoration of the day in which ADONAI gave the Torah to Israel and the mixed multitude, as they stood at the base of Mt. Sinai. Believers of ADONAI YESHUA also know this date as Pentecost, from the Greek pentekoste, meaning 50th. It was on this day, 10 days following ADONAI YESHUA'S ascension to Heaven, that the promised Blessed Holy Spirit of the Living God came to the 70 disciples, as they stood at Solomon's Colonnade, a portion of the Jerusalem Temple. Many believers claim the disciples were speaking from the upper room, in the heart of Jerusalem; however, this area is too small and the streets too narrow for the thousands of people who were reported to have gathered.

The *omer* is a measure of weight, usually of grain. It is about 2.5 litres of seed. When the seed is ground and sifted and sifted again, the measure is about 1.5 litres. Why are we commanded to count the Omer?

This is a time for us to reflect upon our relationship with ADONAI and how we view Him in our lives. This prepares us to recommit ourselves to ADONAI YESHUA, through His Holy Spirit, and continue with the mission He has given us all.

Why ought believers to celebrate the counting of the Omer? This is a time for all of us to think about ADONAI YESHUA and His promise to always be with us, through His Holy Spirit. Although we constantly reflect upon His role in our lives, this is a specific and special time to focus on Him and how we relate to Him. As well, by taking this time to focus on ADONAI YESHUA, we are honouring ADONAI's word to be obedient to His commands.

SHAVU'OT

The Feast of Weeks, *Shavu'ot*, was given to us by ADONAI, as recorded in Leviticus 23. This was the time of the gathering of the wheat harvest and our focus upon ADONAI and His provisions for us. This is a one-day celebration, held on 6 Sivan, the third biblical month, beginning with *Aviv*/Nisan.

Shavu'ot is celebrated by Rabbinic Jews and Messianic believers (Jew and Gentile) with the reading of Torah, at the beginning of 6 Sivan (after sundown), throughout the night, attending a synagogue or congregational meeting place on Shabbat morning, and a festive meal, towards the end of the day. As well, the Book of Ruth is read, while at home. This is a day of rest, so no work is permitted.

FESTIVAL OF SUKKOT

Sukkot, or the Festival of Tabernacles or Booths, comes during the 7th month of the biblical year, Tishrei. This coincides with the fruit harvest. In present day Israel, this harvest involves many exotic fruits, such as pomegranates, bananas, oranges, etc. However, during this age, the usual fruit were grapes, olives and figs. Every community had a winepress and a threshing floor, upon which their fruits and crops were gathered and from which the seed was released.

To recognize the Festival, every family would collect a *lulav*, a combination of a palm frond, a myrtle twig, a leafy branch of a willow tree and the fruit of a citrus tree, called an *etrog*. The myrtle, palm frond and willow branch represented the three most common tree species in Israel, at the time, with the citrus fruit being added when they became plentiful. The three species are bound into one set and, together with the citrus, are waved before ADONAI, while at the synagogue. Below, find an image of a lulav and etrog.

Shavu'ot is recognized by Messianic believers as being the time ADONAI YESHUA will tabernacle with us for 1,000 years. This holy festival is a portion of the 6 appointed times of ADONAI that speak to His relationship with His children as being a marriage.

THE PILGRIMAGE FESTIVALS

There are three pilgrimage festivals Israel is to attend at the Temple. The present tense is used here, since the temple, although it does not presently exist, will be reconstructed in the near future. These festivals are Hag HaMatzot (Festival of Unleavened Bread),

Shavu'ot (Feast of Weeks and Pentecost) and Sukkot (Festival of Tabernacles or Booths). We see this commandment in Deuteronomy 16:16. Each family or clan is to have a representative attend with an offering to display the members' gratitude for ADONAI's provisions.

This concludes our fourth weekly reading.

May the God of Abraham, Isaac and Jacob bless you fully and richly.

Parashah Shoftim (Judges)

Deuteronomy 16:18 to 21:9

Our fifth reading of Sefer D'Varim, the Book of Deuteronomy, covers a wide-ranging set of teachings, from the establishment of just courts to dealing with community sinfulness. Moshe continues with his teachings, before Israel crosses the Jordan River.

Please read the passage focused on here before you engage the text.

Parashah Shoftim (Judges)

Deuteronomy 16:18 to 21:9

Appoint judges and officials for your tribes in all your towns the LORD your God is giving you. They are to judge the people with righteous judgment.

Deuteronomy 16:18

The first portion of this week's reading focuses on the creation of a system of justice for Israel. As we read all through the *Tanakh*, the Hebrew Scriptures, ADONAI is always focused on justice for all His people. In this portion, Moshe teaches his people to appoint judges and justice officials all through the country they occupied, when they cross the Jordan River. Notice verse 20 clearly indicates ADONAI's desire: *Pursue justice and justice alone, so that you will live and possess the land the LORD your God is giving you.* Deuteronomy 16:20.

You may also have noticed the desire for true justice, in ADONAI's command. Read verse 19 carefully - *You are not to distort justice or show favoritism, and you are not to accept a bribe, for a gift blinds the eyes of the wise and twists the words of even the upright.*

As if foreseeing the future, Moshe advised his people to avoid creating worship sites, similar to those of their pagan neighbours, anywhere in the land. This is made very clear, in verse 22 - *and do not set up a sacred pillar; the LORD your God hates them.*

The first command Moshe teaches in Chapter 17 deals with which animal is to be sacrificed to ADONAI. The commandment requires the animal to be free of physical defects or flaws. As this first verse clarifies for us, *that is detestable to the LORD your God.* Deuteronomy 17:1.

Idolatry is another theme of teaching in Deuteronomy. Moshe, in this section of

Chapter 17, focuses on the alien practice of worshipping objects in the sky[36], as avatars for other deities. Anyone in Israel engaging in this practice, was to be brought before the village gates and stoned to death.

However, the trial could only commence, if there were a minimum of two witnesses who observed this practice. The role of a witness also extended to the stoning process, as we read in verse 7, *The witnesses' hands are to be the first in putting him to death, and after that, the hands of all the people. You must purge the evil from you.*

Verses 8 to 13 deal with cases that are too controversial or difficult for the local administration to handle. In these cases, the case in question is to be taken to the Levitical priests and the high court. The verdict that the high court gives is to be followed in its entirety, in accordance with the Torah. The consequence for failure to follow the court's judgment is clearly outlined in verses 12 and 13: *The person who acts arrogantly, refusing to listen either to the priest who stands there serving the LORD your God or to the judge, must die. You must purge the evil from Israel. Then all the people will hear about it, be afraid, and no longer behave arrogantly.*

ADONAI had enabled Moshe to understand the desire for Israel to eventually demand a human king to rule over them. Thus, he taught them, in verse 14 and 15 - *When you enter the land the LORD your God is giving you, take possession of it, live in it, and say, 'I will set a king over me like all the nations around me,' you are to appoint over you the king the LORD your God chooses. Appoint a king from your brothers. You are not to set a foreigner over you, or one who is not of your people.*

Very clearly, although ADONAI disliked the concept of a human king for Israel, He realized such a reality was inevitable, since He understands human nature and human desires. Thus He laid out the requirements for the choosing of a king and for the King's conduct, as we have read verse in 15. Then, in verses 16 to 20, we get a sense of how the king is to perform his duties: *However, he must not acquire many horses for himself or send the people back to Egypt to acquire many horses, for the LORD has told you, 'You are never to go back that way again.' He must not acquire many wives for himself so that his heart won't go astray. He must not acquire very large amounts of silver and gold for himself. When he is seated on his royal throne, he is to write a copy of this instruction for himself on a scroll in the presence of the Levitical priests. It is to remain with him, and he is to read from it all the days of his life, so that he may learn to fear the LORD his God, to observe all the words of this instruction, and to do these statutes. Then his heart will not be exalted above his countrymen, he will*

---

[36] Some translations refer to the heavens, rather than the sky.

not turn from this command to the right or the left, and he and his sons will continue ruling many years over Israel.

The first portion of Chapter 18 Moshe focuses on the status of the Levites, within the communities of Israel. As we are told, ADONAI was the inheritance the Levites received. Read verse1 and 2: *The Levitical priests, the whole tribe of Levi, will have no portion or inheritance with Israel. They will eat the LORD's fire offerings; that is their inheritance. Although Levi has no inheritance among his brothers, the LORD is his inheritance, as He promised him.*

From verse 3 to verse 8, Moshe teaches Israel that the Levites would receive portions of the sacrifices Israel made at the Altar of the Tabernacle. However, they would not share in the harvest of the fields or trees; rather, they would be given what Israel presented as the first fruits of the harvest and the first of the sheared wool of their flocks. Let's read a portion of that, from verses 3 and 4: *This is the priests' share from the people who offer a sacrifice, whether it is an ox, a sheep, or a goat; the priests are to be given the shoulder, jaws, and stomach. You are to give him the firstfruits of your grain, new wine, and oil, and the first sheared wool of your flock.*

A major portion of Chapter 18 focuses on Moshe's teaching Israel to refrain from the practices of the nations surrounding them regarding the occult. Let's read Moshe's teaching in verses 10 to 12: *No one among you is to make his son or daughter pass through the fire, practice divination, tell fortunes, interpret omens, practice sorcery, cast spells, consult a medium or a familiar spirit, or inquire of the dead. Everyone who does these things is detestable to the LORD, and the LORD your God is driving out the nations before you because of these detestable things.*

In addition, Moshe shared with them ADONAI's promise that He would send Israel prophets who would speak His words and guide them on their walk with Him, reminding Israel of His blessings and curses. This promise is found in verses 15 to 22. Let's read a small portion here, from verses 15 and 16: *The LORD your God will raise up for you a prophet like me from among your own brothers. You must listen to him. This is what you requested from the LORD your God at Horeb on the day of the assembly when you said, 'Let us not continue to hear the voice of the LORD our God or see this great fire any longer, so that we will not die!'*

How was Israel to know if a reputable prophet turned and began teaching his own ideas? Moshe answers this question in verses 21 and 22 - *You may say to yourself, 'How can we recognize a message the LORD has not spoken?' When a prophet speaks in the LORD's name, and the message does not come true or is not fulfilled, that is a message the LORD has not spoken. The prophet has spoken it presumptuously. Do not be afraid of him.*

The first 13 verses of Chapter 19 deal with the cities of refuge, their locations and their function. As we have read in these verses, the cities of refuge were to be situated equal distance from each other, throughout the land of Israel. These cities were used to provide a safe haven for those whose actions, while innocent, caused the death of a neighbour. In all there were to be 6 cities of refuge built. Let's read a portion from these verses: *Here is the law concerning a case of someone who kills a person and flees there to save his life, having killed his neighbor accidentally without previously hating him: If he goes into the forest with his neighbor to cut timber, and his hand swings the axe to chop down a tree, but the blade flies off the handle and strikes his neighbor so that he dies, that person may flee to one of these cities and live. Otherwise, the avenger of blood in the heat of his anger might pursue the one who committed manslaughter, overtake him because the distance is great, and strike him dead. Yet he did not deserve to die, since he did not previously hate his neighbor.* Deuteronomy 19:4-6.

Please note that peace amongst the tribes was a primary aim for ADONAI. Thus, in verse 14, He commanded that the boundary markers, separating the tribes' lands, not be touched or moved.

The final 7 verses of Chapter 19 deal with witnesses of a crime. Let's read a portion of these verses: *If a malicious witness testifies against someone accusing him of a crime, the two people in the dispute must stand in the presence of the LORD before the priests and judges in authority at that time. The judges are to make a careful investigation, and if the witness turns out to be a liar who has falsely accused his brother, you must do to him as he intended to do to his brother. You must purge the evil from you.* Deuteronomy 19:16-19. As you read through these verses, you will notice that ADONAI, through Moshe, has clearly stated that malicious prosecution is to be avoided. It was left to the judges to decide if a witness is truthful or a liar. If the first witness is declared a liar, then he is to receive the same punishment as the originally charged person. Let's read those verses again, *The judges are to make a careful investigation, and if the witness turns out to be a liar who has falsely accused his brother, you must do to him as he intended to do to his brother.* Deuteronomy 19:18,19.

The entirety of Chapter 20 deals with Israel's conduct, during periods of warfare. We begin with Moshe teaching his people they are to trust ADONAI only, when they engage an enemy. Moshe knows and exhorts his people to be brave and fight in the knowledge ADONAI is waging battle with them, ensuring victory. Let's read a portion of this exhortation: *When you are about to engage in battle, the priest is to come forward and address the army. He is to say to them: 'Listen, Israel: Today you are about to engage in battle with your enemies. Do not be cowardly. Do not be afraid, alarmed, or terrified because of them. For the LORD your God is the One who goes with you to fight for you against your enemies to give you victory'.* Deuteronomy 20:2-4.

A second lesson to be learned focuses on those men who are exempt from fighting. These include:

a. *Has any man built a new house and not dedicated it? Let him leave and return home. Otherwise, he may die in battle and another man dedicate it.* Deuteronomy 20:5

b. *Has any man planted a vineyard and not begun to enjoy its fruit? Let him leave and return home. Otherwise he may die in battle and another man enjoy its fruit.* Deuteronomy 20:6

c. *Has any man become engaged to a woman and not married her? Let him leave and return home. Otherwise he may die in battle and another man marry her.* Deuteronomy 20:7

d. *Is there any man who is afraid or cowardly? Let him leave and return home, so that his brothers' hearts won't melt like his own.* Deuteronomy 20:8,

thus ensuring all the men who fight for their country and their inheritance are willing, sturdy and courageous enough to engage in battle.

It is interesting that Moshe provides a rationale for these conditions. Let's read that now: *Let him leave and return home, so that his brothers' hearts won't melt like his own.* Deuteronomy 20:8.

The next issue dealt with focuses on approaching enemies and how to deal with them before engaging in battle. Moshe teaches his people they are to seek a peaceful solution first, before engaging in battle. If the enemy engaged in peace talks, the people within the city gates became forced labourous. Let's read that passage: *When you approach a city to fight against it, you must make an offer of peace. If it accepts your offer of peace and opens its gates to you, all the people found in it will become forced laborers for you and serve you.*
Deuteronomy 20:10,11.

If, however, the leaders of the city refused to surrender and desired to fight, Israel was to besiege the city and once having taken it, put all the men to the sword. All the women, children and animals could be taken as spoils of war. The passage is quite explicit: *When the Lord your God hands it over to you, you must strike down all its males with the sword. But you may take the women, children, animals, and whatever else is in the city — all its spoil — as plunder. You may enjoy the spoil of your enemies that the Lord your God has given you.*

Deuteronomy 20:13,14.

There was a caveat ADONAI gave Moshe and which he taught his people. When they crossed the Jordan River and entered their new land, they were to rid the cities of all inhabitants. Here is what Moshe taught, in verses 16 to 18: *However, you must not let any living thing survive among the cities of these people the Lord your God is giving you as an inheritance. You must completely destroy them — the Hittite, Amorite, Canaanite, Perizzite, Hivite, and Jebusite — as the Lord your God has commanded you, so that they won't teach you to do all the detestable things they do for their gods, and you sin against the Lord your God.*

In Deuteronomy 21 Moshe teaches mainly on legal issues. First he addresses the issue of unsolved murders. Without witnesses to testify about the death of an Israelite, Moshe taught his people an alternative approach to removing guilt from them. First, they were to measure the distance from the site of the killing to the nearest town: *If a murder victim is found lying in a field in the land the Lord your God is giving you to possess, and it is not known who killed him, your elders and judges must come out and measure the distance from the victim to the nearby cities.* Deuteronomy 21:1,2.

From the closest city to the killing, the elders and civic authorities would bring a young heifer, unyoked and not used for service. They would bring the heifer to the closest stream where Levites, appointed by ADONAI, would break its neck. At this point, the elders of the city would wash their hands in the stream and declare: *Our hands did not shed this blood; our eyes did not see it. Lord, forgive Your people Israel You redeemed, and do not hold the shedding of innocent blood against them.* Deuteronomy 21:7,8a. This action will absolve the people of that city from the guilt of the killing. This section of the chapter concludes with: *You must purge from yourselves the guilt of shedding innocent blood, for you will be doing what is right in the Lord's sight.* Deuteronomy 21:9.

This is the end of the fifth Weekly Reading

DEEPER UNDERSTANDINGS

JUSTICE

Maintaining justice was and still is a central theme of the Tanakh, the Hebrew Scriptures. We are repeatedly told justice belongs to ADONAI; it is not a human construct. In Torah, for example, every book contains some element of justice in its teaching. In Deuteronomy 16, this teaching comes directly through Moshe advising his people to establish a system of justice that pursues ADONAI's objectives. In verse 18, Moshe emphasises His command with the words, *They are to judge the people with righteous judgment.* There was to be a *Sanhedrin,* or high court, established for each tribe. The judges would appoint officers whose responsibility was to enforce the decisions of the judges and ensure these judgments were carried out. They were also responsible for enforcing standards of honesty in the marketplace and for bringing before the judges any violators of those standards.

There was a danger existing within Israel, that proved accurate as time moved on. The fear was that a collapse of respect for the existing standards would lead to anarchy and the eventual breakdown of the nation. This would also lead to the breakdown of the role of ADONAI's Word.

EQUAL JUSTICE

All too often judges and prosecutors are bribed or show favouritism to those with power and/or prestige or bend over backwards to appease the desires of the less fortunate. In ADONAI's world, justice is and will be seen as well as felt to be equal. No one was above His law and everyone, regardless of rank or wealth, would be treated the same. As we read in Deuteronomy 17:11, Torah provides a strong, firm base and an unchangeable principle that leads us to the Truth.

It would be impossible for a judge to be impartial, if he or she has accepted a bribe; even if they ignore the source of the bribe, they are still malleable by having accepted it. As a result his or her desire to speak justly and fairly will be perverted.

WITNESSES

As we have observed throughout history, many rulers have acted against their citizens on the testimony of only one witness. Torah presented an entirely different approach by asserting that the accounts of two or more witnesses, with a minority of two, was the basis for laying a charge against a citizen. In light of this, a cardinal law of testimony has emerged; that being, the total group of witnesses, two or more, are considered to be one unit. Thus, if only one of them is determined to be untruthful, the entire group of witnesses is to be disqualified.

HIGH COURT JUDGMENTS

The great high court, the Great Sanhedrin, had the authority to resolve all cases and, much like the judgments of a supreme court, were binding even when applied to noted academics, lower court judges and sages. This was a measure to ensure, once more, that the nation of Israel did not devolve into chaos and anarchy when court decisions were disregarded. Thus, the death sentence applied to anyone, regardless of their station. This judgment would apply to even a well-respected judge or academic, who defied the ruling of the Great Sanhedrin. Why was the judgment so harsh?

The Great Sanhedrin was a body created by ADONAI to act on His behalf, in dealing with difficult cases. Their judgments were as if they came from ADONAI and there was no rejecting these. The alternative was, of course, anarchy and disorder. ADONAI is a God of order and will never tolerate disorder or anarchy in His realm.

APPOINTING ISRAEL'S KING

At the time of Deuteronomy, just before Israel passed over the River Jordan, ADONAI was Israel's king. He was the one who controlled their movements and led them into battle. It was He who cared for them and guarded them. However, He also knew they would some day desire a human king, just like the nations around them.

ADONAI knew that if Israel regarded the surrounding nations through their human eyes, they would want to emulate them. And, as we read in 1 Samuel 8:5 - *They said to him, "Look, you are old, and your sons do not follow your example. Therefore, appoint a king to judge us the same as all the other nations have."* Thus then continued the downward slide for Israel. They began to move away from ADONAI.

Knowing that Israel would move in this direction, ADONAI laid out His regulations for the choosing of a king. Thus, the king would be chosen and anointed by ADONAI. The person chosen to be king was to be from one of the tribes of Israel, a citizen of the nation who displayed exceptional leadership skill and qualities, including obedience to His word and humility. The first king of Israel was *Sha'ul,* Saul, son of *Kish* of the Tribe of *Binyamin,* Benjamin.

Conduct of the King

The position of king was not to bring with it extra privileges and undue power. Thus, ADONAI proclaimed that the king of Israel was not to obtain a large number of horses, mainly from Egypt, as horses were to become a sign of wealth.

Another requirement was the forbidding of the king to gather many wives around him. ADONAI knew that wives had a great influence on the hearts and minds of men and He knew if a king gathered many wives around him, he would listen to them and they would draw him astray. The third major command was for the king to make his own copy of the Torah, within the presence of Levitical priests. He was then to read his copy everyday and follow its precepts. Thus, as Moshe explained in verse 20, the king of Israel would not set himself above his people and act arrogantly with them. Of course many of them did, as we have read in the Prophets and the Writings.

The Levites

As we read in Numbers 3:11-13, the tribe of Levi was chosen as the substitutes for the first born males of Israel. Let's read that section: *The LORD spoke to Moses: "See, I have taken the Levites from the Israelites in place of every firstborn Israelite from the womb. The Levites belong to Me because every firstborn belongs to Me. At the time I struck down every firstborn in the land of Egypt, I consecrated every firstborn in Israel to Myself, both man and animal. They are Mine.*

Another reason for their being chosen as Israel's Temple advocates and priests, is found in Exodus 32. Here we read of the Levites functioning as Israel's warrior priests, who killed about 3,000 people who worshipped the golden calf, thus violating the covenant they agreed to earlier. In recognition of their following ADONAI's command, they were declared the direct inheritors of ADONAI's blessings, separate from the other tribes. As we have read, the Levites lived around the Sanctuary, apart from the mass of Israel and the Mixed Multitude.

The priests, *kohanim,* were divided into 8 groups, called 'watches'[37], with each group responsible for the duties performed in the Tabernacle, as we read in 1 Chronicles 24. During their journey through the wilderness, the kohanim did not engage with the community; however, when they entered the land of Israel, they were responsible for teaching the community in which they lived, acting as spiritual leaders, and for guiding

---

[37] Ben Maimon, *The priestly shifts*, Chabad, https://www.chabad.org/library/article_cdo/aid/961434/jewish/Positive-Commandment-36.htm, accessed 30 July, 2024.

their community in the way of Torah. This they did through direct teaching and their personal behaviour.

We are told, for the first time, what the Levites would receive from the sacrifices made on the Altar. As we read from verse 3 of Deuteronomy 18, from each of the animals sacrificed, be they oxen, sheep or goat, the Levites are to receive the shoulder, jowls and stomach. They would also receive the first fruits of the grain, the new wine and the freshly pressed olive oil.

In addition, the Levites would also receive the first of the wool sheering of Israel's flocks. This wool would be spun into thread to make the ordinary clothing of the Levites and, especially, the priests.

Avoid the Occult

When Israel entered the wilderness, they were in lands occupied by nations who had engaged in many practices of the occult. Their parents witnessed the Egyptians practicing 'magic' as part of their religious beliefs. These practices focused on idolatry and were based on man-made decrees. Instead, the people were to rely on ADONAI only for leadership and direction. This included leaning on Him, as they entered an unknown future, rather than asking sooth-sayers to read their fortunes. Relying on Him, through their passionate loyalty and obedience to His leadership, would be the best way for Israel to succeed in the promised land.

Prophets

In this passage of Torah, we find a prophecy of the first coming of ADONAI YESHUA, the LORD JESUS. Indeed, when Moshe said, *The LORD your God will raise up for you a prophet like me from among your own brothers,* he could only be referring to ADONAI YESHUA, as only Moshe and our Messiah had this relationship of openness and humility with ADONAI. Other prophets from among the people would emerge from Israel, as they were needed. As it has been noted elsewhere,[38] there were

---

[38] The 54 male and female prophets of Israel are discussed within the portion of the Hebrew Bible, called the Nevi'im, the Prophets. Those, whose writing appears in Scripture, are listed as the 4 major prophets (Elijah, Ezekiel, Isaiah and Jeremiah) and the 12 minor prophets (Hosea, Joel, Amos, Obadiah, Daniel, Jonah, Micah, Nahum, Habakkuk, Zephaniah, Haggai, Zechariah and Malachi). The difference between major and minor prophet was made for the length of their writing, not their perceived level of respect.

48 male and 7 female prophets recorded in Israel, within the Hebrew Scriptures[39], whose responsibility was to lead Israel according to ADONAI's path.

As well, while in Israel, the people encountered many false prophets, those who professed to teach ADONAI's word but rather taught their own false ideologies and doctrines. When the people came across such false prophets, they were commanded by ADONAI to kill them quickly, so as to reduce the number of people who might be swayed by the false teachings.

CITIES OF REFUGE

In the Middle East, at this time, it was customary for the family of a man killed through accident or deliberately, to seek vengeance by themselves killing the one who caused the death. In His infinite wisdom, ADONAI ordered that 6 cities in Israel be set aside to serve as cities of refuge for those within the region who needed to flee, to avoid the vengeance sought by the dead person's family.

These cities of refuge were originally the cities occupied by the Levites, the priests and Temple workers. The Levites were not given inheritances of land, as were the 12 tribes of Israel. ADONAI was their inheritance and, as such, they were scattered throughout Israel. The 6 cities of refuge, mentioned in Joshua 20:7,8 - *So they designated Kedesh in the hill country of Naphtali in Galilee, Shechem in the hill country of Ephraim, and Kiriath-arba (that is, Hebron) in the hill country of Judah. Across the Jordan east of Jericho, they selected Bezer on the wilderness plateau from Reuben's tribe, Ramoth in Gilead from Gad's tribe, and Golan in Bashan from Manasseh's tribe.*

The incident would be taken to court, the Sanhedrin, and if the killing was ruled accidental, the originally charged would be allowed to live in the city of refuge, until the death of the *Kohen HaGadol,* the High Priest of the Temple. If he left the city of refuge before the high priest died, then the avenger, from the victim's family, was free to exact his revenge.

WITNESS CONSPIRACY

The Talmud, in Sanhedrin 27a, has stated the command from ADONAI defies logic, in that if a second set of witnesses comes forward to dispute the testimony of the first, the evidence of the second set is to be believed, rather than the first.

---

[39] *Ancient Jewish History: List of Jewish Prophets,* Jewish Virtual Library, https://www.jewishvirtuallibrary.org/list-of-jewish-prophets, accessed 30 July, 2024.

The Talmud claims this is a 'novel ruling'[40], since it is virtually impossible to distinguish a lie from the truth, without collaborating evidence. Further, the Talmud declares that the testimonies of both sets of witnesses be set aside, until collaborating evidence is produced to substantiate the correct evidence. However, Torah gives more credibility to the second set of witnesses, rather than the first, even though there is no evidence of truth or falsehood in either set of witnesses.

ISRAEL AT WAR

Guided by ADONAI, Moshe knows his people would tend to see their enemies as having superiority in numbers and, possibly armament; however, to ADONAI they would be insignificant. There would be those within the ranks of the army who are faint of heart and lack the courage to face their enemies. Either due to their situation at home or their own fear of death, these negative thoughts would diminish their effectiveness as warriors and leak into the minds and hearts of their comrades.

Those who were excused from actually fighting were required to assist the army behind the lines. They would be responsible for providing food and water to the troops who were engaged.

The Kohen, responsible for addressing the army of Israel and guiding their minds into war, was chosen specifically for this purpose. He would be at the same level as the Kohen Hagadol.

ADONAI is a merciful God and His mercy is seen in the requirement for Israel to sue for peace before engaging in war. There appears to be disagreement amongst ancient commentators of Torah. Rashi[41] and Raavad[42] claimed only those cities which were not in Israel's inherited lands were to be offered peace, while those Cana'anites within the inherited lands were to be exterminated. On the other side were Rambam and Ramban. Rambam[43] claims Israel was to desire peace with all their enemies. Those who accepted peace were required to pay taxes, engage in some form of national service and accept the 7 Noahide Laws if they were to remain in the land.

Ramban[44] agreed with Rambam regarding the need to offer a peaceful option, especially with the Cana'anites, particularly since they were living in the land occupied by Israel. Indeed, we find in Numbers 21, Moshe & Joshua offered a peaceful solution

---

[40] Rava, Sanhedrin 27a:3, Sefaria, https://www.sefaria.org/Sanhedrin.27a.3?lang=bi, accessed 30 July, 2024.

[41] Rabbi Shlomo Yitzchaqi, 1040-1104, French commentator of Torah and Talmud.

[42] Rabbi Abraham ben David, 1125-1198, commentator of Torah, from Provence, France.

[43] Moses ben Maimon, 1138 – 1204, a Sephardic philosopher in Spain. Known as Maimonides, he wrote the 13 principles of Jewish law, which are used today by most orthodox rabbis.

[44] Rabbi Moshe ben Nachman, 1194 – 1270, his belief was the Talmud was unquestionable in its decisions and discussions. Thus, if the rabbis over-ruled ADONAI's command, it was over-ruled.

to King Sichon, whose kingdom existed within and outside Israel's inherited land. Unfortunately this peace was not accepted and Sichon's nation was defeated in battle.

Since its inception, in 1948, the modern state of Israel has fought 18 wars, involving one or more countries around it. With the exception of the current Hamas war, 2024, which is ongoing, Israel has been successful in defeating all these atrocities.

CANA'ANITES IN ISRAEL'S LAND

Once more we may see dissonance among commentators, regarding the process of dealing with Cana'anites living in Israel's land. The key passage in Deuteronomy 20 is verse 15: *This is how you are to treat all the cities that are far away from you and are not among the cities of these nations.* Many of the commentators argued that this passage indicated those Cana'anite cities within the confines of Israel's land were to receive the option of a peace treaty. Ramban claimed that the offer of a peace settlement was applied to everyone, including the Cana'anites. If they accepted the peace offer, they were to convert to Judaism and be taught how to worship ADONAI. If they did not agree to the peace offer, every man, woman and child was to be exterminated.

More recently, Jehoshua M. Grintz[45], of Tel Aviv University, wrote Y'hoshua was

---

[45] Grintz, J., *The treaty of Joshua with the Gibeonites*, Journal of the Oriental American Society, 86:2, 1966, Pp.113-126.

deceived by the Gibeonites, who persuaded him to not exterminate them from their land, as they lived far from Israel. However, the Gibeonites lived within Israel. Having made the oath to secure them, Y'hoshua and his leaders could not go back on their word, even if deceived.

Unfortunately, as we learn through the Hebrew Scriptures, particularly the Book of Judges, many Cana'anites remained in Israel and did seduce Israel to engage in idolatry. As a result, many disasters came upon Israel.

UNSOLVED MURDER

In ancient Israel, any killing affected the health of the total community. Given that every gathering of people also housed sin, it was imperative that the event be noticed publically. Thus, without witnesses to testify about the killing, everyone in the nearest community must have shared in the guilt. To remove that guilt from members of the community, the ritual outlined in verses 5 to 8 of Chapter 21 would be used to absolve the citizens of the closest city from guilt.

Eben Ezra[46] believed that the elders of a community held a degree of responsibility for any unwitnessed killing, since their community was a home for sin.

Rambam[47] believed that making the killing public knowledge would have brought many people to the public ceremony, allowing the elders to gain more information about the killing. This may have enabled the elders to uncover the murderer.

This ends our fifth weekly reading.

May you be fully and richly blessed by the God of Abraham, Isaac and Jacob.

---

[46] Eben Ezra, born 1092, died 1167, a Spanish poet and writer. He published many commentaries on Torah.
[47] Moses ben Maimon (Maimonides), ibid.

Parashah Ki Tetze (When you go out)

Deuteronomy 21:10 to 25:19

In our sixth weekly reading, we find Moshe continuing his teaching of ADONAI's word to Him. We begin with his teaching that allows soldiers to take foreign women captured in battle as wives.

Please read the passage focused on here before you engage the text.

PARASHAH KI TETZE (WHEN YOU GO OUT)

DEUTERONOMY 21:10 TO 25:19

When you go to war against your enemies and the LORD your God
hands them over to you and you take some of them prisoner, and if
you see a beautiful woman among the captives, desire her, and want
to take her as your wife, you are to bring her into your house.

Deuteronomy 21:10-12

In verses 10 to 14, Moshe teaches Israel regarding the fair treatment of non-Israeli women captured during battle. ADONAI allowed soldiers to take captured women from their conquered cities to be their wives, as Moshe taught in verse 11: *. . . you see a beautiful woman among the captives, desire her, and want to take her as your wife.* He also taught about the care that the capturing soldier is to provide his captive, as we read in verses 12 and 13a: *you are to bring her into your house. She must shave her head, trim her nails, remove the clothes she was wearing when she was taken prisoner, live in your house, and mourn for her father and mother a full month.* After this time of mourning is complete, the soldier may marry his captive. However, if she displeases him in any way, he may have her leave the home, without recrimination, as we read in verse 14: *Then if you are not satisfied with her, you are to let her go where she wants, but you must not sell her for money or treat her as merchandise, because you have humiliated her.*

The second issue Moshe addressed with Israel was the treatment of the sons from second wives. Listen to his teaching, as found in verses 15 to 17: *If a man has two wives, one loved and the other unloved, and both the loved and the unloved bear him sons, and if the unloved wife has the firstborn son, when that man gives what he has to his sons as an inheritance, he is not to show favoritism to the son of the loved wife as his firstborn over the firstborn of the unloved wife. He must acknowledge the firstborn, the son of the unloved wife, by giving him two shares of his estate, for he is the firstfruits of his virility; he has the rights of the firstborn.* However, what might happen with the instance of a rebellious son?

Many parents can relate to the story of the rebellious son. Indeed, the story of the prodigal son (Luke 15:11-32) is taught often in congregations around the world. Israel also had its share of rebellious sons. Moshe taught his people a process of dealing with such a stiff-necked, stubborn individual, in verses 18 to 21 of Chapter 21. Let's read from that section: *If a man has a stubborn and rebellious son who does not obey his father or mother and doesn't listen to them even after they discipline him, his father and mother must take hold of him and bring him to the elders of his city, to the gate of his hometown. They will say to the elders of his city, 'This son of ours is stubborn and rebellious; he doesn't obey us. He's a glutton and a drunkard.' Then all the men of his city will stone him to death. You must purge the evil from you, and all Israel will hear and be afraid.*

The final two verses of Chapter 21 deal with the capital punishment of hanging. Those who are hung from a tree, or from the wood taken from a tree, are to be cut down before the day's end. Let's read that passage: *If anyone is found guilty of an offense deserving the death penalty and is executed, and you hang his body on a tree, you are not to leave his corpse on the tree overnight but are to bury him that day, for anyone hung on a tree is under God's curse. You must not defile the land the LORD your God is giving you as an inheritance.* Deuteronomy 21:22,23. If you have read John 19:38, you will realize this rule was in effect, when YESHUA was crucified. His body was removed from the execution stake and taken for burial before the sun set.

In Chapter 22, Moshe returns to teaching care to one's neighbours. His example is found in verses 1 to 4: *If you see your brother's ox or sheep straying, you must not ignore it; make sure you return it to your brother. If your brother does not live near you or you don't know him, you are to bring the animal to your home to remain with you until your brother comes looking for it; then you can return it to him. Do the same for his donkey, his garment, or anything your brother has lost and you have found. You must not ignore it. If you see your brother's donkey or ox fallen down on the road, you must not ignore it; you must help him lift it up.* Thus the theme of Leviticus 19:18 - *Do not take revenge or bear a grudge against members of your community but love your neighbor as yourself,* is continued in this teaching.

The next teaching focuses on cross-dressing. Read what Moshe teaches about this:

A woman is not to wear male clothing, and a man is not to put on a woman's garment, for everyone who does these things is detestable to the LORD your God. Deuteronomy 22:5. I have explored these thoughts more deeply, below, but for now it is important to note ADONAI's views of men and women have been consistent throughout the ages. He does not wish for there to be a blurring of the lines between the genders.

The next set of teachings is within the context of kindness and compassion. The first deals with removing a chick from a nest, while the mother is present. Read with me this teaching: *If you come across a bird's nest with chicks or eggs, either in a tree or on the ground along the road, and the mother is sitting on the chicks or eggs, you must not take the mother along with the young. You may take the young for yourself, but be sure to let the mother go free, so that you may prosper and live long.* Deuteronomy 22:6,7. As we all know, the food we eat comes from both the plants which are grown and the animals that roam. Kindness extends even to the animals we eat.

The next teaching, *If you build a new house, make a railing around your roof, so that you don't bring bloodguilt on your house if someone falls from it.* Deuteronomy 22:8, is clearly designed to prevent Israelis from accidently falling from rooves of houses. Most Israeli houses carried flat roofs, since the weather was consistently warm. Many had drains for rain water, when it fell, to be collected inside the house, where it was stored in a cistern.

The next teaching focuses on planting crops. ADONAI's teaching has always been not to mix grains in the same field. Similarly, in this teaching, we find: *Do not plant your vineyard with two types of seed; otherwise, the entire harvest, both the crop you plant and the produce of the vineyard, will be defiled.* Deuteronomy 22:9.

Even the use of animals had to be conveyed to Israel. This teaching forbids mixing oxen and donkeys, used to plow fields: *Do not plow with an ox and a donkey together.* Deuteronomy 22:10.

Consistent with the commands against mixing, ADONAI has ordered that threads of wool and linen not be woven together to produce one garment. Read this with me, in verse 11: *Do not wear clothes made of both wool and linen.*

The final teaching in this section of Chapter 22, deals with the wearing of *tzitziyot,* fringes at the bottom of the outer garments worn by Israeli men: *Make tassels on the four corners of the outer garment you wear.* Deuteronomy 22:12.

Verses 13 to 20 focus on the proof of a bride's virginity. Verse 13 introduces this issue clearly. Let's examine it - *If a man marries a woman, has sexual relations with her, and comes to hate her, and accuses her of shameful conduct, and gives her a bad* name, saying, 'I married this woman and was intimate with her, but I didn't find any evidence of her virginity,' the young woman's father and mother will take the evidence of her virginity and bring it to the city elders at the gate. Deuteronomy 22:13-15. The virginity of brides was a most important aspect of marriage. You may wish to read Matthew 1:18-25, to read how Yosef reacted when he realized Miriam was pregnant. If a bride was not a virgin, she would be considered a prostitute and unfit for marriage. This issue of proving the virginity of the bride is discussed below.

There was a consequence for making a false statement about a bride's virginity. In verses 18 and 19, we read - Then the elders of that city will take the man and punish him. They will also fine him 100 silver shekels and give them to the young woman's father, because that man gave an Israelite virgin a bad name. She will remain his wife; he cannot divorce her as long as he lives. However, if the accusation is true, then a different process is set in place, as we read in verses 20 and 21: But if this accusation is true and no evidence of the young woman's virginity is found, they will bring the woman to the door of her father's house, and the men of her city will stone her to death. For she has committed an outrage in Israel by being promiscuous in her father's house. You must purge the evil from you. The evidence used to prove virginity is a cloth which the mother of the bride places on the wedding bed, before the marriage is consummated. During the consummation, blood from the ruptured hymen will flow onto the cloth. The next morning, the mother of the wife will collect the cloth and keep it, in case an accusation comes forth.

The last portion of Chapter 22 deals with infidelity among married men. Moshe was required to teach Israel that infidelity was not to be tolerated in Israel, as it was in other societies. In the first instance, if a man and a woman had extra-marital sex, both could be stoned to death, if discovered. Let's read that passage - If a man is discovered having sexual relations with another man's wife, both the man who had sex with the woman and the woman must die. You must purge the evil from Israel. Deuteronomy 22:22. If a virgin is discovered having sex with a man, other than her betrothed, while in a town or city, she could have been stoned to death, because she did not cry out: If there is a young woman who is a virgin engaged to a man, and another man encounters her in the city and has sex with her, you must take the two of them out to the gate of that city and stone them to death—the young woman because she did not cry out in the city and the man because he has violated his neighbor's fiancée. Deuteronomy 22:23,24. However, if this is a case of rape outside the city, the woman would be spared, as no one was around to hear her (Deuteronomy 22:25,26) In this case, only the man must be killed, if he is discovered.

If a man rapes a virgin, when discovered he must pay the girl's father 50 shekels and marry her. He is not permitted to ever divorce her. The final instruction of Deuteronomy 22 states: *A man is not to marry his father's wife; he must not violate his father's marriage bed.* Deuteronomy 22:30. We have also read this in Leviticus 18:8: *You are not to have sexual relations with your father's wife; that is your father's prerogative.*

In the first portion of Deuteronomy 23, verses 1 to 8, Moshe taught his people those who were excluded from the Tabernacle: *No man whose testicles have been crushed,* verse 1; *whose penis has been cut off,* verse 1; *No one of illegitimate birth,* (called a mamzer*), may enter the LORD's assembly; none of his descendants, even to the tenth generation, may enter the LORD's assembly,* verse 2; *No Ammonite or Moabite may enter the LORD's assembly; none of their descendants, even to the tenth generation, may ever enter the LORD's assembly,* verse 3. However, both Edomites and Egyptians could attend the assembly with Israel, as Moshe taught in verses 7 and 8 - *Do not despise an Edomite, because he is your brother. Do not despise an Egyptian, because you were a foreign resident in his land. The children born to them in the third generation may enter the LORD's assembly.*

As we may see, ADONAI's perspective of cleanliness extended to Israel's camp, as well as their persons. As we read in verse 15, *For the LORD your God walks throughout your camp to protect you and deliver your enemies to you; so your encampments must be holy. He must not see anything improper among you or He will turn away from you,* the camp was a holy place. Let's read a portion of this section, to understand this rulings implications: *When you are encamped against your enemies, be careful to avoid anything offensive. If there is a man among you who is unclean because of a bodily emission during the night, he must go outside the camp; he may not come anywhere inside the camp. When evening approaches, he must wash with water, and when the sun sets he may come inside the camp.* Deuteronomy 23:9-11. The reason for this command is discussed below; however, we know Moshe was teaching ADONAI's command from Leviticus 15. In this chapter we are told that Moshe taught his people how to dispose of their bodily waste, as we read in verses 12 and 13 - *You must have a place outside the camp and go there to relieve yourself. You must have a digging tool in your equipment; when you relieve yourself, dig a hole with it and cover up your excrement.* ADONAI Himself explains why this is important, in verse 14, *For the Lord your God walks throughout your camp to protect you and deliver your enemies to you; so your encampments must be holy. He must not see anything improper among you or He will turn away from you.*

Verses 15 and 16 of Chapter 23, speak about the treatment of run-away slaves: *Do not return a slave to his master when he has escaped from his master to you. Let him live among you wherever he wants within your gates. Do not mistreat him.* This issue is discussed more fully, below.

Verses 17 and 18, condemn cult prostitution. Let's read these verses: *No Israelite woman is to be a cult prostitute, and no Israelite man is to be a cult prostitute. Do not bring a female prostitute's wages or a male prostitute's earnings into the house of the Lord your God to fulfill any vow, because both are detestable to the Lord your God.*

In verses 19 and 20, Israelites were not allowed to charge their brothers interest on loans, while they could for loans to foreigners: *Do not charge your brother interest on money, food, or anything that can earn interest. You may charge a foreigner interest, but you must not charge your brother interest, so that the Lord your God may bless you in everything you do in the land you are entering to possess.*

Verses 21 to 23, teach Israel to ensure their vows are completed in a timely manner; however, there was no punishment if a vow wasn't made: *But if you refrain from making a vow, it will not be counted against you as sin.* Deuteronomy 23:22. If a vow is made and not kept, this would be considered a sin: *If you make a vow to the Lord your God, do not be slow to keep it, because He will require it of you, and it will be counted against you as sin.* Deuteronomy 23:21. A question arises from this portion; it would be valuable to address it here and now. Does this mean that a vow not voiced but thought would not be considered a sin?

To answer this question, we need to search through Scripture. In 1 Samuel 16:7b we read: *Man does not see what the Lord sees, for man sees what is visible, but the Lord sees the heart.* Then we read in Mark 7:21-23: *For from within, out of people's hearts, come evil thoughts, sexual immoralities, thefts, murders, adulteries, greed, evil actions, deceit, promiscuity, stinginess, blasphemy, pride, and foolishness. All these evil things come from within and defile a person.* Thus, we know that our thoughts begin in our hearts, our subconscious or second mind. This not only applies to our evil thoughts but also to our righteous thoughts. The answer to the question, then is yes, a vow in our heads only is as binding as a vow spoken.

The final portion of Deuteronomy 23, verses 24, 25, focus on gathering food from a neighbour's field: *When you enter your neighbor's vineyard, you may eat as many grapes as you want until you are full, but you must not put any in your container. When you enter your neighbor's standing grain, you may pluck heads of grain with your hand, but you must not put a sickle to your neighbor's grain.*

Chapter 24 begins with a teaching on divorce. Moshe begins with a hypothetical issue - *If a man marries a woman, but she becomes displeasing to him because he finds something improper about her, he may write her a divorce certificate, hand it to her, and send her away from his house.* Deuteronomy 24:1. He then completes this teaching by elaborating on the condition mentioned in verse 1: *If after leaving his house she goes and becomes another man's wife, and the second man hates her, writes her a divorce certificate, hands it to her, and sends her away from his house or if he dies, the first husband who sent her away may not marry her again after she has been defiled, because that would be detestable to the LORD. You must not bring guilt on the land the LORD your God is giving you as an inheritance.* Deuteronomy 24:2-4. You may remember ADONAI YESHUA, the LORD JESUS, discussing this issue with a group of Sadducees, as recorded in Matthew 19:3-11. Here is just a snippet of this conversation: *Moses permitted you to divorce your wives because of the hardness of your hearts. But it was not like that from the beginning. And I tell you, whoever divorces his wife, except for sexual immorality, and marries another, commits adultery.* Malachai 2:16, Matthew 19:8,9 and Luke 16:19.

Verse 5 provides relief for a newly married couple, when the man is required to fight in a war: *If a man has recently married his wife, he is not to be subject to military service; he is to be free of external obligations and left at home for one year to make his new wife happy.*

The next four verses, 6-9, focus on issues of safeguarding life, specifically a security debt and persons who are left without means for providing for family. The first issue is fair and equal measure: *Do not take a pair of millstones or an upper millstone as security for a debt, because that is like taking a life as security.* Deuteronomy 24:6. The second deals with kidnapping a neighbour or community member: *If a man is discovered kidnapping one of his Israelite brothers, whether he treats him as a slave or sells him, the kidnapper must die. You must purge the evil from you.* Deuteronomy 24:7. And the third addresses the issue of defiling diseases: *Be careful in a case of infectious skin disease, following carefully everything the Levitical priests instruct you to do. Be careful to do as I have commanded them. Remember what the LORD your God did to Miriam on the journey after you left Egypt.* Deuteronomy 24:8,9.

Chapter 25 begins with a teaching on fairness and mercy, in dealing out punishment for committed crimes. If the accused was found guilty and sentenced to the punishment of flogging, he, or she presumably, was to receive no more than 40 strokes. Let's read a bit of this: *If the guilty party deserves to be flogged, the judge will make him lie down and be flogged in his presence with the number of lashes appropriate for his crime. He may be flogged with 40 lashes, but no more. Otherwise, if he is flogged with more lashes than these, your brother will be degraded in your sight.* Deuteronomy 25:2,3.

Verse 4, *Do not muzzle an ox while it treads out grain,* is also an important lesson for all of us today. This is discussed in greater detail, below.

The next set of teachings, found in 25:5-12, focus on preserving the family line. Here is a sample: *When brothers live on the same property and one of them dies without a son, the wife of the dead man may not marry a stranger outside the family. Her brother-in-law is to take her as his wife, have sexual relations with her, and perform the duty of a brother-in-law for her. The first son she bears will carry on the name of the dead brother, so his name will not be blotted out from Israel.* Deuteronomy 25:5,6.

As appears to be Moshe's style of teaching, verses 11 and 12 deal with the punishment of a wife who comes to aid her husband, when he is attacked by another person: *If two men are fighting with each other, and the wife of one steps in to rescue her husband from the one striking him, and she puts out her hand and grabs his genitals, you are to cut off her hand. You must not show pity.* It appears she may grab any other part of the attacker's body but the genitalia are to be hands-free.

The next teaching addresses the use of honest weights and measures. Let's read a portion: *You must not have two different weights in your bag, one heavy and one light. You must not have two differing dry measures in your house, a larger and a smaller.* Deuteronomy 25:13,14. This issue appears frequently in Torah, as we read of it in Genesis 18, Leviticus 19 and Proverbs 16. Verse 16 provides a clear rationale for the practice of using honest weights and measures: *For everyone who does such things and acts unfairly is detestable to the LORD your God.*

The final teaching in this week's reading is found in verses 17 and 18. Here, Moshe teaches his people to: *blot out the memory of Amalek under heaven. Do not forget.* Deuteronomy 25:19. We read this in Exodus 17:8 - *At Rephidim, Amalek came and fought against Israel.* They did not meet Israel directly but attacked the stragglers at the rear of the community, which was considered a devious strategy at that time.

This is the conclusion of our sixth weekly reading.

Deeper Understandings

Treatment of Captured Women

Here is but one example of the mercy ADONAI extended to foreign women captured by Israeli soldiers. They were to be given all the rights and privileges of Israeli married women. They were not to be enslaved and were given the responsibility of the home. Their roles, along with their Israeli counterparts, included the preparation of daily meals, cleaning the homes, raising the children and preparing the daily and special offerings to ADONAI.

However, foreign women, from the nations surrounding and even within Israel, presented a critical danger to Israel. Many, if not most, refused to relinquish their idols and house-gods. Thus, their families were led into adultery, designated as fornication with idols.[48]

There is a lengthy procedure that the captured woman must follow before she becomes the soldier's wife. This procedure, described by the rabbis in Talmud[49], allows for the heat of passion to dissipate, so that the soldier will grow weary of waiting and will free the woman, before he has married her.

If an Israeli man wished to have his foreign wife leave him, in order to marry another, all he had to do was open the door and provide her with the resources to establish her new life. As Scripture shares with us, letting a foreign wife go into the world alone is a humiliating experience for the woman. Thus, she must not be sold nor diminished in any other way, because of the humiliation created by the 'divorce'. Deuteronomy 21:14.

What does this say to us today? These instructions focus on the captured woman being a human being. Thus, the waiting period allows for men to gain control of their natural desires (lust) and regard the situation more calmly. Clearly, the captured woman would be humiliated by being let go, so there is some compensation due to her by the man. This relates to sex before marriage. Once a couple becomes engaged, they are required to wait until the 'husband' has a place for them to live before they are fully married. Thus sex waits until that time. If 'the bloom falls off the rose' and the relationship sours, the woman is not 'damaged' and would be able to find a husband.

---

[48] Ackerman, S., *Women in Ancient Israel and the Hebrew Bible*, Oxford Research Encyclopedia, 2016, https://doi.org/10.1093/acrefore/9780199340378.013.45 Accessed 06 July, 2023.
[49] Kiddushin 68b.

The Unloved Son

ADONAI never gave Israel the right to practice polygamy; however, due to their hard-hearted attitudes, polygamy was tolerated. In order to enforce standards within the practice, Moshe introduced the standard of unique rights, responsibilities and privileges of the first born, regardless of the birth mother. Thus, if the first-born son comes from the unloved wife, that son was to be given first-born status. Preferential treatment was not to be shown to the second-born son if he emerged from the loved wife. Interestingly enough, this rule was not followed with the birth of Ishmael (Genesis 17:15-22).

Interestingly enough, the situation of the second born having the birthright of the first born may be seen with Reuven and Yosef. As we read in Genesis 49, Reuven took Ya'akov's concubine to bed, thus humiliating his father. Through this action, Reuven lost his birthright and it was transferred to Yosef. Why was Ishmael not given the birthright of the first born? We know Adonai told Avraham that the birthright needed to come from Sarah; however, we also know, as we read in Genesis 16 and 21, both Hagar and Ishmael taunted Avraham and Sarah. These acts of rebellion were enough for Ishmael to lose his birthright, which was passed onto Yitzchak.

The Rebellious Son

Discipline in ancient times was quite different from practices today. I have heard many parents complain that their children run the family or that they have great difficulty disciplining their children. Perhaps parents in ancient times experienced the same conditions. Moshe, in an attempt to quell the rebellion within Israel, may have instituted this regulation, with the implicit support of ADONAI, in order to ensure rebellion would never again emerge from his people. He certainly had experienced enough rebellion in his time as leader to justify implementing some measure to put an end to this treacherous aspect of life in Israel.

Yes, it appears that every generation, from the earliest of times, has dealt with the antics of the rebellious son. It appears ADONAI has little patience with these rebels who flagrantly fight against the control of their parents. As we have read in the pages of Torah, it was from those who rebelled against the teachings of ADONAI, through Moshe, the entire community of Israel was forced to wander through the wilderness for a total of 40 years.

In order to ensure that the second generation of Israelites did not have the same ending as the first, ADONAI commanded stiff consequences for the sons of Israel who refused to listen to the direction of their parents. As is mentioned in Deuteronomy

21:21, *You must purge the evil from you, and all Israel will hear and be afraid.* ADONAI's message to Israel is very clear; His standards of conduct are far superior to those of society. Should children be able to behave as they choose, following their inherent emotions, Israelite society would crumble and children would become anathema to their parents.

There is a clear message for us today. Many parents today would rather be friends with their teenage children, rather than their parents. Disciplining a child is essential for its correct positioning in the world. The Book of Proverbs clearly relates to the role of parents in the lives of their children. For example, Proverbs 13:24 shares with us, *The one who will not use the rod* (guidance) *hates his son, but the one who loves him disciplines him diligently.*

Many organizations providing parenting advice, such as Parenting Nerd,[50] suggest the approach of dealing with the problem, not the child. Thus tackling the problem the child is facing may alleviate the need for strong discipline.

HANGING FROM A TREE

This regulation, given to Israel by Moshe, continued for quite some time; as we have read in the B'rit Chadashah, also called the New Testament, when YESHUA was crucified on the wooden stake. His disciples, Nicodemus and Joseph of arimathea, received permission from Pilate to remove Him from the curse of being hanged and placed His body into a tomb, as we read in all four of the Canonical Gospels.

Rashi[51] indicated the practice of hanging individuals is disgraceful to ADONAI Himself, since His people were made in His image. The practice may be seen as the twin brother of a king being hanged. Those passing by might have seen the king himself being hanged and receive this with great sorrow.

CARE FOR NEIGHBOURS

The Torah, as well as throughout the Tanakh, the Hebrew Scriptures, focuses on taking care of one's neighbours. We find, in Matthew 22:39, *The second* (Great Command) *is like it: Love your neighbor as yourself.*

There is much debate about feeding one's animals on Shabbat or on a Holy Day, such

---

[50] Hicks, E., Parenting Nerd, https://parentingnerd.com. Accessed 10 July, 2023.
[51] Rashi, Shlomo Yitzchaki, 1040 to 1105, Medieval French Rabbi, authored commentaries on the Talmud and Hebrew Scripture.

as Yom Kippur. The *Gemara Shabbat*[52] establishes that on Shabbat it is permissible to feed those animals who are reliant on their owner for substance. However, on Shabbat one must not feed another's animals or animals that are running wild.

The question of feeding one's neighbour's animals has been raised. While there appears to be no direct answer to the question, the *Shulchan aruch*, Orach Chaim[53] 324:11 indicates that animals which are dependent upon humans for their welfare are to be fed on Shabbat.

HOMOSEXUALITY

The issue of homosexuality is clearly detailed throughout Scripture. In Torah, for example, we find in Genesis 19 the story of homosexuality within the city of Sodom, where lot lived with his family; then in Leviticus 18:22 and 20:13, ADONAI commanded Moshe to tell his people that homosexual behaviour would not be tolerated in Israel. In 1 Kings 14:24, we read of the cultic male prostitutes, serving in Israel, contrary to ADONAI's commands.

Within the B'rit HaChadashah, we find many portions teaching against homosexual activity. In Romans 1:26,27, we read, *This is why God delivered them over to degrading passions. For even their females exchanged natural sexual relations for unnatural ones. The males in the same way also left natural relations with females and were inflamed in their lust for one another. Males committed shameless acts with males and received in their own persons the appropriate penalty of their error.* This is very clear statement of ADONAI's standard for heterosexual relationships, as outlined in Genesis 2:20-25: *The man gave names to all the livestock, to the birds of the sky, and to every wild animal; but for the man no helper was found as his complement. So the LORD God caused a deep sleep to come over the man, and he slept. God took one of his ribs and closed the flesh at that place. Then the LORD God made the rib He had taken from the man into a woman and brought her to the man. And the man said: This one, at last, is bone of my bone and flesh of my flesh; this one will be called "woman," for she was taken from man. This is why a man leaves his father and mother and bonds with his wife, and they become one flesh. Both the man and his wife were naked yet felt no shame.*

---

[52] Gemara Shabbat 155b:
[53] The Shulchan Aruch has been labelled 'the Code of Jewish Law', although it literally means 'Set Table'. It was written in 1563 by Joseph Karo. The Shulchan Aruch principally focused on Sephardic Jews. Orach Chaim, 'Way of Life', deals with issues related to daily ritual observances.

In ancient Cana'an, dating back before 1900 BCE[54], homosexuality was tolerated, if it was conducted between consenting adults. Only Israel had concrete laws which forbade the practice of homosexual activity completely. The earliest known code of conduct, the Code of Hammurabi[55], mentioned nothing about homosexual behaviour. Later Assyrian rulings discussed homosexual behaviour, with some statutes condoning and others condemning the practice, in certain situations.

Also in these ancient times, both men and women were allowed and even encouraged to be cult prostitutes. As we read on the website "The Bible Says[56]," such practices were designed to heighten religious fervour and to flatter the gods so crops and flocks would be fertile.

TAKING A CHICK OR EGG

I'm sure many of us, age 50+, have heard the saying, 'Don't kill the goose that laid the golden eggs.' This homily is to be found in Moshe's teaching regarding taking the eggs or chicks found in nests as food and leaving the mother bird alone. There will always be more eggs produced; However, killing the mother and taking her as food will ensure she lays no more eggs. God's compassion extends to even the smallest of His creations.

PLANTING TWO GRAINS IN THE SAME FIELD

In the ancient Middle East, with its lack of sophisticated equipment and machinery, multi-cropping would have been a problem. All harvesting was conducted by hand and it could have been difficult to differentiate which grain was being harvested. Additionally, when one crop was ready to harvest, such as barley, another, wheat, was still growing. Thus during harvesting, while one crop was being properly taken, the other might be severely damaged, ruining a potential food crop. Thus, ADONAI ordered Moshe to provide this teaching of planting only one crop in a field, monocropping.

There are also symbolic and spiritual reasons associated with this command. For example, with the introduction of seeds other than grape seeds to a vineyard would be pollution of the vineyard. This would symbolize the introduction of worshiping other deities than our ADONAI[57].

---

[54] Wenham, G.J., *The Old Testament attitude towards homosexuality*, Expository Times, 102.9, 259-363, 1991.

[55] Code of Hammurabi, the sixth Amorite king of the ancient Babylonian Empire, lived from 1810 – 1750 BCE and reigned between 1792 and 1750 BCE.

[56] The Bible Says, *Deuteronomy 23:17-18 meaning*, The Bible Says Biblical Commentary, https://thebiblesays.com/commentary/deut/deut-23/deuteronomy-2317-18/, accessed 20 March 2024.

[57] Clark, A., *The Holy Bible*, Eaton & Mains, New York, 1986, found in Guzik, D., *Enduring Word, Commentary*, Enduring Word Bible Commentary Deuteronomy Chapter 23, accessed 26 June 2024.

This situation was discussed in Matthew 13:24-30, where ADONAI YESHUA shared His parable about the wheat and the tares (weeds) together. When the wheat was ready to be harvested, the tares were gathered first and thrown into the fire, then the wheat was harvested.

The prohibition on planting different grains the same field applies in our time also. In our case, this command applies to our raising of children. As parents, we are responsible for the first planting of seed (knowledge, understanding) into the mind of a child. Then, throughout the child's life, parents are responsible for nurturing, modeling, disciplining and living out the Word of Adonai. Young children are voracious learners. They learn quickly and absorb everything presented to them, until they become thinking beings and begin questioning. Thus, as parents we must plant fertile seed into their minds – the word of ADONAI. His principles of living, treating others and focusing attention upon Him needs to begin being taught before the child can speak. When other thoughts, the ways of the world, begin to make their approach, your children will have the understanding and the weapons to protect them and be able to choose what is true and good.

MIXING PLOW ANIMALS

Not all of us have used animals, instead of machines, in plowing fields. I would not hesitate to say not one of us reading this volume have used an ox or a donkey in plowing. However, in ancient Israel, these were the only two sources of power for plowing fields. The prohibition of using oxen and donkeys together was to save the farmer untold headaches. Clearly oxen are more powerful than donkeys and more compliant. Donkeys tend to be stubborn and, when yoked with an ox, could slow down the plowing. Donkeys could also help steer the plowing off course, pulling either to the left or right, creating an unevenly plowed field; hence the command not to commit these animals to the same yoke. This teaching may also be seen as a metaphor for the marriage of a believer to an unbeliever. In this case, the unbeliever may pull the believing spouse away from the love of ADONAI and move into apostasy. Of course the opposite is also true, where the believing spouse may bring the unbelieving spouse closer to ADONAI, thus further increasing the Kingdom of ADONAI.

2 Corinthians 6:14-16 speaks of this matter, in relation to humans. Let's read some of this portion: *Do not be mismatched with unbelievers. For what partnership is there between righteousness and lawlessness? Or what fellowship does light have with darkness?* Oftentimes, as may be seen today, the non-believing partner may draw the believing partner away from her/his faith. However, the believing partner may encourage and assist the nonbelieving partner, as a catalyst, to accept ADONAI YESHUA as her/his personal Messiah.

Do Not Despise an Edomite

In verses 7 and 8 of Chapter 23, we are given the command to Moshe that the Edomites are not to be harmed by Israel. You may recall, Edom came from Esav, the brother of Ya'akov. As such, Esav was the grandchild of Avraham, with whom ADONAI made an everlasting covenant. However, Edom, as a nation, hated Israel and became the symbol of all the nations that held this animosity towards ADONAI'S children. The Nation of Edom was conquered by the Nabatean arabs in the 5th Century BCE. Some of them fled into southern Y'hudah, during the time of the Maccabees, becoming known as the Idumeans. When they began to fight against Israel, they were destroyed by Israel and ceased to exist[58].

Mixing Wool and Linen

In ancient Israel, while the Tabernacle and Temple were existing, only the kohanim, the priests, were permitted to wear garments constructed of wool or linen (Exodus 28, 39). These were men considered to be of higher integrity than the common man. As

---

[58] *WHAT HAPPENED TO THE EDOMITES?*, Enduring Word, https://enduringword.com/what-happened-to-the-edomites-qa-for-december-10-2020/#top, accessed 25 June 2024.

such, their garments, used in ceremonies, were not to be duplicated by the common man. Lois Tverberg, writing in Our Rabbi Jesus,[59] states: *Both the priestly garments and the tabernacle weavings were a combination of wool and linen. The priest's white undergarment was linen, and the brightly colored vestment was wool. So it was prohibited for laypersons to dress in the same way.*

WEARING TZITZIYOT

The command to wear tzitziyot, tassels, is to be found in Numbers 15:38-40. These tassels were to be attached to the bottom of a male's outer garment, usually a cloak, and would, presumably, trail along the ground. ADONAI's command to wear tzitziyot carries with it the prescription for reading and remembering His commands, spread throughout the Torah. Thus, when an Israelite male was to make a decision, he would have the tzitziyot to help him remember ADONAI's commands, ensuring he made the correct decision, given the circumstances. However, this is not the only purpose for wearing tzitziyot; following the incident at Sheetim, when Israel 'played the harlot' with women of Moab, worshipping ba'al of Peor, Numbers 25:1-4, Adonai ordered all Israeli men to wear Tzitziyot to remind them of Adonai's commands.

Today, we have no idea how many Jewish men wear tzitziyot today; there are no statistics available. Tzitziyot are commonly worn by Orthodox Jews and by many Messianic believers, Jew and Gentile. Although Scripture does not provide a use for wearing Tzitziyot, other than this is ADONAI's command, many believers see it as a guide to Torah. This is particularly useful when making a decision. If the mind can be brought back to Torah, the guide for a decision is present. Personally, Torah has been very helpful for me, as I have made many decisions, throughout my days as a believer.

How do we wear tzitziyot today? Most Jews wear what is known as *tallit katan,* or the 'little tallit', with the tallit being the prayer shawl worn by men (and some women) during Shabbat service and on special occasions. The tallit katan is a single garment, with tassels on its four corners, under the outer clothing – a shirt or sweater. A full tallit may also be worn. Many Messianic believers, Jew and Gentile, wear tzitzit from the belt-loops of the pants, rather than wearing a tallit. Messianic believers are advised to always wear their tzitiyot inside their outer clothes.

---

[59] Tverberg, L., *What's so wrong with mixing wool and linen*, <u>Our Rabbi Jesus</u>, July 2, 2013, <u>https://ourrabbijesus.com/articles/whats-so-wrong-with-mixing-wool-linen/</u>, accessed 19 July, 2023.

Proof of Virginity

In the ancient Middle East, it was normal for men to marry virgins. Any woman or girl who had extra-marital sex was considered a prostitute. Her chances of being married were close to nil.

Usually the discussion of marriage would take place between the fathers of the couple. The arrangements focused on the dowry, provided by the woman's family to the groom's, as well as the bride gift, paid by the groom's family. The bride gift, also known as a *mohar,* at one time might have been considered a ransom amount, freeing the daughter from the family. The mohar morphed into the dowry provided by the groom to the bride.

In order to prove their daughter was a virgin, the mother placed a small piece of cloth in the bridal bed. The same night or next morning the mother would collect the cloth and keep it, in case the husband claimed his wife was not a virgin.

The punishment for the wife not being a virgin was quite severe. The crime was considered to be quite evil. Once there was sufficient proof of prostitution, more than there not being any hymen blood on the wedding cloth, the wife would be taken outside the city gates, where the husband would throw the first stone. Then, other members of the community would stone the woman to death.

If the husband made a false accusation, attempting to be released from the marriage but keeping the dowry, he would be fined a significant amount of money, depending on his resources, and chastened for his jealousy. In addition, he would be required to maintain his marriage with the woman he intended to abandon.

Male Infidelity

Is it possible that the Bible displays a double standard, a different standard towards women as it does towards men? Before we get into that, it is important for us to place the question into its cultural homeland. Often in Scripture we read of both adultery and fornication. These two words did not have the same meaning in ancient times. Adultery meant a husband or a wife had sexual relations with someone other than their spouse. In most cultures, such as ancient Rome, adultery was not tolerated, as it disrupted the social order. Werner Eck[60], in his research into ancient Rome, wrote,

Further, at the beginning of his reign as Princeps, Octavian (Augustus) set the agenda for the type of citizen he wished to see in the Empire. To this end he reformed and

---

[60] Eck, W., *The age of Agustus*, 2nd Edition, <u>Blackwell Publishing</u>, Oxford, 2011, Pp. 101-103.

introduced new laws about marriage and adultery. Adultery became a crime that could be tried in the criminal court and if found guilty, the adulterers would be exiled.

In ancient Israel, adultery could be punishable by death of both parties, as we read in Leviticus 20. However fornication was permitted. Fornication, at this time, was men having more than one wife, usually a slave, with whom he could raise a larger family. As we read in Genesis 30, Jacob was given his two wives' slave girls as his new wives.

Thus, ancient Jewish law prescribed that adultery was a capital offence, as opposed to exile. Later, in the apostolic portion of Jewish history, fornication was outlawed, as we read in the letter Ya'akov, James, wrote to the Gentile believers in areas outside Israel, as we read in Acts 15: *Therefore, my opinion is that we should not put obstacles in the way of the Goyim who are turning to God. Instead, we should write them a letter telling them to abstain from things polluted by idols, from fornication, from what is strangled and from blood. For from the earliest times, Moses has had in every city those who proclaim him, with his words being read in the synagogues every Shabbat.* Acts 15:19-21. However, this was not a new ordinance. From the time of King Solomon later into the second Temple period, prophets were sharing God's word with the people of Israel and Judea to abstain from having slave wives, especially since they tended to draw their husbands into idolatry. We read of this in 1 Kings 11, when Solomon accumulated 700 wives and 300 concubines, disobeying Adonai's command to only have one wife. In Ezra 9, Israel was warned not to allow their sons to marry foreign women or their daughters foreign men, who worshipped other deity, again an instance of forbidding the mixing and its consequences. Doing this also drew Israel into idolatry – moving away from Adonai.

Incest in Ancient Israel

Living in such close quarters, it would seem possible for close relatives to develop a fondness for each other. ADONAI knew this to be a problem and taught early in the wandering that *None of you is to approach anyone who is a close relative in order to have sexual relations,* Leviticus 18:6 and Leviticus 20:11-21. Each of these chapters provides a list of close relatives with whom both men and women are to abstain from having sexual contact. The penalty for both parties caught in such a liaison was death if they were observed and two witnesses came forward.

Excluded from the Tabernacle

In Chapter 23 of *Sefer HaD'Varim*, the Book of Deuteronomy, we are told there were 4 classes of people who were excluded from the Tabernacle and the later Temple: 1. Those whose testicles have been crushed; 2. those whose penises have been cut off; 3. Those who are of illegitimate birth (mamzer) and 4. Those who belong to the Ammonite or Moabite nations. Just what does the phrase 'excluded from the tabernacle' mean?

David Guzik[61] shares with us that the assembly of Adonai refers to the leaders of Israel, who represent the congregation, elders and officers. He further emphasizes these exclusions were not "from the religious life of Israel but from the political life of the nation." This may seem strange but the Temple was the focal point of both the religious and political life of the community. Thus, if someone was excluded from the Tabernacle/Temple, this could have been both a religious and political reaction to someone's action.

As we know, ADONAI's standards of perfection apply not only to the animals that were to be sacrificed but also to those who appeared before Him in the Tabernacle and the Temple. Those whose testicles have been damaged are not considered 'perfect', in ADONAI's eyes. This may seem contrary to our 21st Century minds; we must remember ADONAI's standards are much higher than are ours. ADONAI is perfection; thus, when He asks for perfection, He demands perfection. Our obligation is to obey, even if we don't understand. The same standard applies to those who are of illegitimate birth. But, you think or say, it's not their fault their parents engaged in illicit sexual activity. True, but remember ADONAI's command, in Numbers 14:18 - *The LORD is slow to anger and rich in faithful love, forgiving wrongdoing and rebellion. But He will not leave the guilty unpunished, bringing the consequences of the fathers' wrongdoing on the children to the third and fourth generation.*

---

[61] Guzik, D., *Deuteronomy 23,* Enduring Word, Enduring Word Bible Commentary Deuteronomy Chapter 23, accessed 26 June, 2024.

> *If the children do not learn from their parents sinful behaviours, they will carry the sin into their lives. Once the child, at any age, repents and asks ADONAI for forgiveness, their sin will be removed. God does not carry on the sins of the father onto the child, if the child repents.*

Why have the Ammonites and Moabites been excluded from the Tabernacle and Temple, while the Edomite and Egyptian are allowed to enter? Remember the Edomite Nation emerged from Esau, Ya'akov's brother. Even when there was a falling out between the brothers, family is very important to ADONAI. Thus, Edom was recognized as Israel's brother. This, however, does not explain why Egyptians were allowed to enter. After all, Israel was enslaved by Egypt.

Scripture provides no clear rational for allowing Egyptians in the Tabernacle, except the line, *Do not despise an Egyptian, because you were a foreign resident in his land. The children born to them in the third generation may enter the LORD's assembly.* Deuteronomy 23:7b,8. archeological evidence[62], though, indicates Egyptians and other nations in the area, had constructed tabernacles very similar in structure to the one ADONAI directed Moshe to build. Was Moshe cognizant of these? Would this have made it easier to pass this information on to others? We probably will never know; however, with this knowledge, we may see ADONAI having worked with the nations around Israel, earlier in history.

---

[62] Armstrong, D., *The Tabernacle: Egyptian & Near Eastern Precursors*, <u>Biblical evidence for Catholicism</u>, 08 September, 2021, <u>https://www.patheos.com/blogs/davearmstrong/2021/09/the-tabernacle-egyptian-near-eastern-precursors.html</u>, accessed 04 August, 2023.

Bodily Emissions

As we have seen elsewhere (Leviticus 15 and 17) ADONAI viewed life having come from blood; thus, blood was forbidden to be eaten. The same measure applied to bodily emissions. All bodily emissions come from blood, either directly or through manipulation. Thus, if a man or woman had an emission, while asleep, they needed to go outside the camp and wash themselves clean of the emission. As we are told, in Leviticus 15:8, *he is to wash his clothes and bathe with water, and he will remain unclean until evening.* We go back to ADONAI's standards of conduct. When a man or woman have emissions, originating with blood, they are contaminated. If they remained in the camp, the camp is contaminated and ADONAI would not be able to walk through it, as He said he would, in Numbers 2:2. For the same reason, ADONAI required all bodily waste to be placed in specially dug latrines, in areas where people did not normally walk.

ADONAI came to the camp of Israel, to speak with Moshe in the Tent of Meeting, located in the center of the camp.

In ancient times, when there was a relatively small number of humans on earth[63], excrement was either thrown away, into rivers and streams, in specially dug latrines or used for fertilizer. As settlements increased in size, bodily waste often was thrown directly into streets and laneways.

Returning Run-Away Slaves

As we have read in Torah (Exodus 21; Leviticus 25) and in other places (Colossians 4), slaves or bondservants were to be treated fairly. Beating a slave to death was forbidden, as we read in Exodus 21:20,21 - *When a man strikes his male or female slave with a rod, and the slave dies under his abuse, the owner must be punished. However, if the slave can stand up after a day or two, the owner should not be punished because he is his owner's property.* As explained by Eliazer Diamond[64], beating disobedient slaves was very common in ancient Middle Eastern societies. However, ADONAI told Moshe to teach His people that Israel was to be separated from other peoples. Thus,

---

[63] Author Unknown, *FLUSHED AWAY: Sewers throughout history flushed away: Sewers through history*, <u>Science Museum, London</u>, U.K., 02 February, 2021. <u>https://www.sciencemuseum.org.uk/objects-and-stories/everyday-wonders/flushed-away-sewers-through-history#:~:text=10%2C000%20years%20ago%2C%20when%20around,became%20a%20more%20significant%20problem</u>. Accessed 04 August 2023.

[64] Diamond, E., *Do not turn away, then and now*, <u>Jewish Theological Seminary</u>, New York, 09 September, 2019; <u>https://www.jtsa.edu/torah/do-not-turn-away-then-and-now/</u>, accessed 16 August, 2023.

slaves could be disciplined, with a non-lethal rod, often shepherd's crook. However, if the slave died, the one who beat the slave was to be punished.

Diamond further contends that Torah's decree on returning slaves to their master was based on moral and ethical grounds. He writes, *The escaped slaves standing before us have risked life and limb to flee their homeland and find protection in ours. Only the sting of the master's lash would have been reason enough to face the dangers and uncertainties of the journey. In granting these slaves asylum the Torah declares here, as it does elsewhere (see* Exod. 21, 20–21; 26–27*), that while slavery is countenanced, harsh and abusive treatment of slaves is not.*[65]

CULT PROSTITUTION

In the ancient Middle East, the only form of prostitution available was to be found at the temple of the society's deity. In ancient Israel, prostitution was quite visible, with prostitutes covering their faces, while waiting by city gates or along the road. We read of two such prostitutes, Tamara (Genesis 38) and Rahab (Joshua 2). However, Torah warns the Levites becoming involved with prostitutes (Leviticus 21), while the Tanakh warns Israelites about allowing their daughters to become prostitutes (1 Kings 3; Proverbs 7; Isaiah 23; Jeremiah 3).

As we read in Sefer HaB'midbar, the Book of Numbers 25:1-5, the leaders of Midian used their cult prostitutes to infiltrate Israel as a way of bringing ADONAI's curses upon them, when Bala'am was unable to complete his task (Numbers 25). As we read in Numbers 25, they were all destroyed but only after many in Israel were turned away from ADONAI.

INTEREST ON LOANS

Israelites were warned about charging interest on loans to other Israelis. ADONAI told Moshe, who taught Israel, *you must not charge your brother interest.* A loan, at this time, was considered an act of kindness to assist a brother out of poverty. Charging interest would only exacerbate the problem. This is taught in Exodus 22, Leviticus 25 and Deuteronomy 23. Thus, only interest-free loans could be offered to Israelites by their brothers. Unfortunately, this law is not enforced today.

---

[65] Diamond, E., Op.Cit.

Making Vows

Vows in Ancient Israel were made before ADONAI, who became a witness. This made making a vow a most solemn event. Thus, not keeping or breaking a vow was considered then, and is still now, a sin against ADONAI. However, if one found himself in a vow that was foolish and hurtful, he could remove himself from it, as we read in Proverbs 6:1-5 - *My son, if you have put up security for your neighbor or entered into an agreement with a stranger, you have been trapped by the words of your lips -- ensnared by the words of your mouth. Do this, then, my son, and free yourself, for you have put yourself in your neighbor's power: Go, humble yourself, and plead with your neighbor. Don't give sleep to your eyes or slumber to your eyelids. Escape like a gazelle from a hunter, like a bird from a fowler's trap.* You may recall the vow made by Jephthah, in Judges 11, where he promised ADONAI, *Jephthah made this vow to the LORD: "If You will hand over the Ammonites to me, whatever comes out of the doors of my house to greet me when I return in peace from the Ammonites will belong to the LORD, and I will offer it as a burnt offering.".* Judges 11:30,31. As we learned, what emerged from the door was not an animal or a man but Jephthah's daughter.

Prohibition – Stealing Neighbour's Grain

In Deuteronomy 23:24,25, we find Moshe teaching from Leviticus 19:18 - *Do not take revenge or bear a grudge against members of your community, but love your neighbor as yourself; I am Yahweh.* This prohibition applied only to Israelites. When Israel conquered other nations, they were allowed to take their grain and vines as part of their spoils of war. However, many ancient and contemporary rabbis maintained Israel must refrain from taking spoils of war, as this would be *a grave desecration of God's name.*[66]

Divorce

The issue of divorce amongst Israel appears not to have been settled. ADONAI does not view divorce as appropriate in any marriage, as He stated in Malachi 2:16 - *So watch yourselves carefully, and do not act treacherously against the wife of your*

---

[66] Author Unknown, *The spoils of war in Jewish law*, Mosaic, 19 February, 2019. https://mosaicmagazine.com/picks/religion-holidays/2019/02/the-spoils-of-war-in-jewish-law/, accessed 17 August, 2023.

*youth. If he hates and divorces his wife," says the L*ORD* God of Israel, "he covers his garment with injustice," says the L*ORD* of Hosts. Therefore, watch yourselves carefully, and do not act treacherously.* At that time and forward, marriage was and still is a covenant, which could be broken only due to adultery. However, Jewish law today allows men and women to divorce their spouses with or without a recognized reason. According to the paper, Jewish attitude towards divorce[67], *Under Jewish law, a man can divorce a woman for any reason or no reason. The Talmud specifically says that a man can divorce a woman because she spoiled his dinner or simply because he finds another woman more attractive, and the woman's consent to the divorce is not required. In fact, Jewish law requires divorce in some circumstances: when the wife commits a sexual transgression, a man must divorce her, even if he is inclined to forgive her.*

Lawrence Goodman[68], investigating women's roles in divorce states, *And even with the increased flexibility, there remain several hundred Hasidic and modern Orthodox women every year who become agunot, Hebrew for chained -- as in a woman chained to her husband and stuck in a marriage from which he cannot or will not release her.* It seems, then, women are not treated equitably with men, in the issue of divorce.

Except in certain cases of misconduct by the wife, a man who divorces his wife is required to pay her substantial sums of money, as specified in the ketubah (marriage contract). In addition, Jewish law prohibits a man from remarrying his ex-wife after she has married another man.[69]

RELIEF FROM MILITARY SERVICE

ADONAI, in His infinite wisdom, recognized certain constraints upon men who were needed for military service but were also needed at home. Verse 5 of Chapter 24 is one of these constraints. Others included the following, as we read in Deuteronomy 20: *The officers are to address the army, 'Has any man built a new house and not dedicated it? Let him leave and return home. Otherwise, he may die in battle and another man dedicate it. Has any man planted a vineyard and not begun to enjoy its fruit? Let him leave and return home. Otherwise he may die in battle and another man enjoy*

---

[67] Author Unknown, *Jewish attitude towards divorce*, Judaism 101, https://www.jewfaq.org/divorce, accessed 07 August, 2023.

[68] Goodman, L., A feminist guide to Jewish divorce, Brandise Now, December 8, 2018.

[69] Author Unknown, Op. Cit.

its fruit.…. The officers will continue to address the army and say, 'Is there any man who is afraid or cowardly? Let him leave and return home, so that his brothers' hearts won't melt like his own. Deuteronomy 20:5-8. Moshe taught this before Israel crossed the Yarden River to begin their conquest of the land.

SAFEGUARDING LIFE

There are three primary principles in Torah: love ADONAI with all our hearts, minds and strength; love our neighbours (community) as ourselves and safeguard life. It is the latter that may need to be examined. Obviously, if we see someone in difficulty we would be willing to help. But what about someone in discomfort? Does that have the same impact upon us?

The principle of pikuach nefesh, **פקוח נפש**, sanctity of life, means saving a soul or preservation of human life beyond anything else. Rabbi Simon Glustrom[70] shares with us, "Most of Jewish law can be and should be set aside in order to avoid endangering a person's health or safety." Thus, Torah requires us to safeguard the lives of those in difficulty. The rabbis, in the Talmud (Yoma 95b), have discussed a number of conditions relating to safeguarding lives. What emerges of significance from this discussion is the underlying principle, *If one is seized by a ravenous hunger, he may be given to eat even unclean things until his eyes are lightened,* indicating that even on Yom Kippur, Day of Atonement, the holiest day in the Messianic calendar, outside Shabbat, one <u>must</u> break the fast, if self or another is in difficulty and needs help.

In Deuteronomy 24, the issue discussed is the specific skin disease, tzara'at, an affliction caused by the bearing of sin, often the sins of gossip and slander. As we read in Numbers 12:9,10, Myriam contracted tzara'at, when she and Aharon criticized Moshe about his marrying a Cushite woman and perhaps from being jealous of Moshe's position and special relationship with ADONAI. Why would Moshe remind Israel and us of his sister's illness?

The issue of gossip and slander has always been a major concern and common practice in almost all cultures and in all times. In Judaism, especially in the ancient days, when there was a heightened spirituality, tzara'at was often seen when people engaged in gossip and slander. With the case of tzara'at, involving the cohanim was most important since they knew the process for dealing adequately with this condition. Failure to approach the priests when this illness occurred, could put one's life in jeopardy. Some would say that the absence of tzara'at today is a blessing.

---

[70] Glustrom, S., *Saving a Life*, <u>My Jewish Learning</u>, <u>https://www.myjewishlearning.com/article/saving-a-life-pikuach-nefesh/</u>, accessed 27 June 2024.

Tzara'at itself is not a medical problem; there are no symptoms other than white patches on the body. There is not pain or disability associated with the condition. This leads us to conclude it is solely a spiritual condition brought about by sin.

Fairness and Mercy in Punishment

We have spent a good deal of space on the topics of fairness and mercy; however, these topics are discussed quite a bit in Torah. Dignity and self-worth are key to the safeguarding of life. Punishment or consequences for crimes committed against one's neighbour or community come appropriately to those convicted, through the fair and merciful judgment of a group of men chosen specifically for this purpose. When the punishment or consequence is administered, it is incumbent upon the judges to ensure that the dignity and self-worth of the individual is maintained, even though he or she is also a criminal. We should wonder if these principles are at play today.

Paying Workers their due

Clearly, the sentence, *Do not muzzle an ox while it treads out grain,* may be seen as a metaphor for the principle of paying those who serve ADONAI by doing His work here on earth. Rav, Sha'ul, the Apostle Paul, uses this understanding in 1 Corinthians 9:1-12, as he writes about the right of all missionaries to receive remuneration for the efforts they put in, as he writes in verses 11 and 12: *If we have sown spiritual things for you, is it too much if we reap material benefits from you? If others have this right to receive benefits from you, don't we even more?* His final comment, verse 13, directly pertains to us, in this age - *In the same way, the Lord has commanded that those who preach the gospel should earn their living by the gospel.*

Preservation of the Line

The Talmud, in Kiddushin 68b, clearly states that Jewish people should not marry others outside of Judaism. If they do, the pagan must convert to Judaism; otherwise both would be subjected to the penalty of death.

This precept was very clearly based on Moshe's teaching, as found in Deuteronomy 25:5,6. Even then, ADONAI foresaw the day when Jewish men and women would look outside their tribes and nation for others to wed. The fear underlying this directive was not only the dilution of the nation of Israel but also, and perhaps more importantly, the breakdown of our worship of ADONAI as our only God. And we may see this as being valid; in the United States, for example, those Jewish people who identified as being with the Jewish community varied from 20% to 70% in different cities.[71]

Thus, Moshe's teaching of the widow of a Jewish man should marry his dead husband's brother, in order to preserve the family line, was a direct attempt to preserve the sanctity of Judaism throughout the ages.

WOMEN GRABBING MEN'S GENITALIA

In the ancient world family was the most important aspect of community. Men were given status by the number of children they sired. If a woman grabbed a man's genitalia, they could be damaged so he could not longer sire children. In the ancient world, this was a grave sin and had to be addressed harshly. Thus Moshe taught his people that in such a situation the woman's hand, used to grab the man's genitalia, should be severed from her body.

HONEST WEIGHTS AND MEASURES

This teaching clearly refers back to Leviticus 19:18b - *love your neighbor as yourself.* Stealing through the use of dishonest weights and measures was common throughout the nations of this time period. Israel was to be different from other nations, as she was the nation of ADONAI. Moshe taught this ruling to reinforce his ongoing teaching of being holy, as ADONAI commanded Israel.

DESTROYING AMALEK

As we learn from extra-biblical sources, the Amalekites were descended from Esau's line. Esau was hated by ADONAI, as we have read in Malachai 1:2,3 - *Even so, I loved Jacob, but I hated Esau.* The Amalekites were considered the cruelest and harshest of the tribes of the Edomites. All through the books of Scripture, from Exodus to the Book of Esther, the Amalekites were a thorn in the side of Israel. In 1 Samuel 15:1-3, we read: *Samuel told Saul, "The LORD sent me to anoint you as king over His people Israel. Now, listen to the words of the LORD. This is what the LORD of Hosts says: 'I witnessed what the Amalekites did to the Israelites when they opposed them along*

---

[71] Pergola D., *Jewish identity, assimilation and continuity*, The A. Harmon Institute of Contemporary Judaism, 2002, p. 14.

the way as they were coming out of Egypt. Now go and attack the Amalekites and completely destroy everything they have. Do not spare them. Kill men and women, children and infants, oxen and sheep, camels and donkeys.'" Unfortunately, as we find, reading on, Saul failed to complete the task assigned him. He was disqualified from the role of King of Israel and David was chosen in his stead.

This concludes our sixth weekly reading.

May the God of Abraham, Isaac and Jacob bless you fully and richly.

Parashah Ki Tavo (When You Come)

Deuteronomy 26:1 to 29:9

In our seventh weekly reading of Sefer D'Varim, the Book of Deuteronomy, we find Moshe continuing his teaching ADONAI's life instructions to the children of Israel.

Please read the passage focused on here before you engage the text.

Parashah Ki Tavo (When You Come)

Deuteronomy 26:1 to 29:9

*When you enter the land the L*ord *your God is giving you as an inheritance, and you take possession of it and live in it, you must take some of the first of all the land's produce that you harvest from the land Yahweh your God is giving you and put it in a container. Then go to the place where the L*ord *your God chooses to have His name dwell. When you come before the priest who is serving at that time, you must say to him, 'Today I acknowledge to the L*ord *your God that I have entered the land the L*ord *swore to our fathers to give us.*

Deuteronomy 26:1-3

In this portion of Deuteronomy, Moshe begins by teaching two important procedures to all of Israel, including the Levites and the foreigners living amongst them. The first of these is the presentation of the firstfruits offering of the crops grown throughout the year, to ADONAI, through the Kohen. Moshe's teaching included what each Israelite farmer was to say when he presented his offering to ADONAI. Here is a sample of his teaching: *My father was a wandering aramean. He went down to Egypt with a few people and lived there. There he became a great, powerful, and populous nation . . . He led us to this place and gave us this land, a land flowing with milk and honey. I have now brought the first of the land's produce that You, L*ord*, have given me.* Deuteronomy 26:5, 9,10.

The second teaching of the chapter deals with the giving of a tenth of the produce to those in need, the widow, the orphan, the Levite and the foreigner. Here is a portion of what Moshe taught: *When you have finished paying all the tenth of your produce in the third year, the year of the tenth, you are to give it to the Levite, the foreigner, the fatherless, and the widow, so that they may eat in your towns and be satisfied.*

Deuteronomy 26:12. As we read in Deuteronomy 14, at the end of the harvest festival, held at the end of the festival of Sukkot, all Israeli farmers and herdsmen were to bring a tenth of their produce and the first born of their herds to the place ADONAI has chosen for His Temple, to share with the people of the communities.

Moshe then taught Israel what they are to say to ADONAI, as they present their offering. Here is a portion: *Then you will say in the presence of the Lord your God: I have taken the consecrated portion out of my house; I have also given it to the Levite, the foreigner, the fatherless, and the widow, according to all the commands You gave me. I have not violated or forgotten Your commands. I have not eaten any of it while in mourning, or removed any of it while unclean, or offered any of it for the dead. I have obeyed the Lord my God; I have done all You commanded me.* Deuteronomy 26:13,14.

The final portion of the chapter consists of Moshe's summary of the covenant ADONAI cut with Israel at the base of Mount Sinai. Here is a sample: *And today the Lord has affirmed that you are His special people as He promised you, that you are to keep all His commands, that He will elevate you to praise, fame, and glory above all the nations He has made, and that you will be a holy people to the Lord your God as He promised.* Deuteronomy 26:18,19.

Chapter 27 begins with the command to write Torah on large stones, covered with plaster. Let's read a portion of this: *Moses and the elders of Israel commanded the people, "Keep every command I am giving you today. At the time you cross the Jordan into the land the Lord your God is giving you, you must set up large stones and cover them with plaster. Write all the words of this law on the stones after you cross to enter the land the Lord your God is giving you, a land flowing with milk and honey, as Yahweh, the God of your fathers, has promised you.* Deuteronomy 27:1-3. The stones were to be transported to Mt. Ebal, north of Jerusalem in Samaria. Here they were to be in the creation of an altar of uncut stones, to be used for fellowship offerings to ADONAI. Here is a sample: *When you have crossed the Jordan, you are to set up these stones on Mount Ebal, as I am commanding you today, and you are to cover them with plaster. Build an altar of stones there to the Lord your God—you must not use any iron tool on them. Use uncut stones to build the altar of the Lord your God and offer burnt offerings to the Lord your God on it. There you are to sacrifice fellowship offerings, eat, and rejoice in the presence of the Lord your God.* Deuteronomy 27:4-7

The remainder of Chapter 27 focuses on the curses that were to befall upon Israel, when they stopped following the commands Moshe taught his people, as he received them from ADONAI. Let's read a portion:

> 'The person who makes a carved idol or cast image, which is
> detestable to the LORD, the work of a craftsman, and sets it up
> in secret is cursed. And all the people will reply, 'Amen!'
> The one who dishonors his father or mother is
> cursed. And all the people will say, 'Amen!'
> The one who moves his neighbor's boundary marker
> is cursed. And all the people will say, 'Amen!'
> The one who leads a blind person astray on the road
> is cursed. And all the people will say, 'Amen!'
> The one who denies justice to a foreigner, a fatherless child,
> or a widow is cursed. And all the people will say, 'Amen!'
> . . .
> The one who secretly kills his neighbor is cursed.
> And all the people will say, 'Amen!'
> The one who accepts a bribe to kill an innocent person
> is cursed. And all the people will say, 'Amen!'
> Anyone who does not put the words of this law into practice is cursed.
> And all the people will say, 'Amen!' Deuteronomy 27:15-19; 24-26.

The entire focus of Chapter 28 is on the blessings for and curses for not following ADONAI's life instructions, as found in Torah. Let's review the blessings.

If Israel obeyed ADONAI's instructions, then the nation would be placed in a favoured position compared to other nations and separated or set apart for Him. Let's read a portion of this blessing:

> You will be blessed in the city and blessed in the country. Your
> descendants will be blessed, and your land's produce, and the offspring
> of your livestock, including the young of your herds and the newborn of
> your flocks. Your basket and kneading bowl will be blessed. You will be
> blessed when you come in and blessed when you go out. Deuteronomy
> 28:3-6.

As we read in verse 7, ADONAI promised to protect Israel from her enemies, as long as the people obeyed His commands. As we read in verse 10:

Then all the peoples of the earth will see that you are called by Yahweh's name, and they will stand in awe of you.

Verse 13 contains an important blessing for Israel:

The LORD will make you the head and not the tail; you will only move upward and never downward if you listen to the LORD your God's commands I am giving you today and are careful to follow them.

The final pronouncement, concerning ADONAI's blessings on Israel, is to be found in verse 14:

Do not turn aside to the right or the left from all the things I am commanding you today, and do not go after other gods to worship them.

The vast majority of Chapter 28 deals with the curses ADONAI planted on Israel, for her disobedience. Verses 15 to 19 provide an overview of these curses. Let's take a look:

But if you do not obey the LORD your God by carefully following all His commands and statutes I am giving you today, all these curses will come and overtake you: You will be cursed in the city and cursed in the country. Your basket and kneading bowl will be cursed. Your descendants will be cursed, and your land's produce, the young of your herds, and the newborn of your flocks. You will be cursed when you come in and cursed when you go out.

Reading through the detail, which I urge you to do, you will find just what did happen to Israel when the Assyrians, the Babylonians and the Romans attacked and captured Jerusalem and the Israelites in the area.

Verse 37 presents a particularly haunting image - *You will become an object of horror, scorn, and ridicule among all the peoples where the LORD will drive you.*

All through history, Jewish people have been the subject of scorn, ridicule and hatred amongst the nations of the world.

There are only 9 verses of Chapter 29, in this week's reading. These verses remind Israel of the blessings ADONAI gave Israel when they made their exodus from Egypt. Let's read this portion:

> *These are the words of the covenant the Lord commanded Moses to make with the Israelites in the land of Moab, in addition to the covenant He had made with them at Horeb. Moses summoned all Israel and said to them, "You have seen with your own eyes everything the Lord did in Egypt to Pharaoh, to all his officials, and to his entire land. You saw with your own eyes the great trials and those great signs and wonders. Yet to this day the Lord has not given you a mind (or heart) to understand, eyes to see, or ears to hear. I led you 40 years in the wilderness; your clothes and the sandals on your feet did not wear out; you did not eat bread or drink wine or beer—so that you might know that I am Yahweh your God. When you reached this place, Sihon king of Heshbon and Og king of Bashan came out against us in battle, but we defeated them. We took their land and gave it as an inheritance to the Reubenites, the Gadites, and half the tribe of Manasseh. Therefore, observe the words of this covenant and follow them, so that you will succeed in everything you do. Deuteronomy 29:1-9.*

This ends our seventh Weekly Reading.

DEEPER UNDERSTANDINGS

FIRST FRUITS

In the Biblical calendar there are three firstfruits festivals, Chag HaMatzot, Shavuot and Sukkot. Chag HaMatzot, or Feast of Unleavened Bread, is held sometime in late March, early April, where no bread product with yeast may be eaten for a full seven days; Shavuot, or Festival of Weeks, is held in the spring, 50 days from the Festival of Matzot, when the wheat harvest occurs; and Sukkot, Festival of Tabernacles, may be found in the fall. These three festivals are known as the pilgrimage festivals, as

Hebrew males are to meet at the Temple to offer their firstfruits. It is highly likely this firstfruits festival is Shavuot, coinciding with the wheat harvest. Each of these festivals is governed by *mitzvot* or commandments, which indicate how the festival is to be conducted. The website, 'Your Jewish Journey', operated by BJE[72], offers 3 explanations for mitzvot. The first is *mishpatim*, commandments of justice that are logical and self-evident. The second is *edot* or testimonials. These are the rules of Jewish festivals, commemorating important events in Jewish history. The third is *chukkiim*, meaning statutes or decrees; they have no discernable rationale and are the ultimate test of faith.

Although the Feast of Unleavened Bread (Hag HaMatzot) is not part of Passover, over the centuries it has been combined. However, ADONAI has ordained that it be considered a separate festival.

Notice the three important moments in time mentioned in the testimony offered by the giver of the gifts: the first recognizes the seminomadic wanderings of the Jewish ancestors, notably Abraham, who was promised by ADONAI to be the progenitor of many nations; the second brings to mind the slavery of Hebrews in Egypt and the miraculous response by ADONAI, who heard their cries and, using Moshe, rescued them and the third is the gift of Cana'an, which ADONAI promised to Abraham.

This annual recitation helped keep Israel's history alive in the minds of people. This annual celebration also is a compelling articulation of Israel's faith.

Tithing the Tenth

Every three years, farmers in Israel are to present a tenth of their produce, crops and animals, to those less fortunate, widows, orphans and the homeless poor. As well, they were to supply the Levites with a tenth of their produce on an annual basis, in order to sustain them. I use the present tense, because the command has not been abolished, even though the Temple is no more. When the third Temple is constructed, the command will come into full effect, again.

The tithe was designed to be for ADONAI and was to be given to the Levites in the Temple. This tithe, given every three years, was directed to be given not to ADONAI but to those in need. Thus even the poor would be cared for.

---

[72] BJE – A Jewish Board of Education, for Jewish children not attending Jewish schools. Operating primarily in Australia.

As you may know, in the Millenium Kingdom, every nation will need to send representatives to Jerusalem for each of the Pilgrimage Festivals. Failure to do so will result in a loss of rain for that nation for a full year. You may read this in Zechariah 14:16.

BLESSINGS FOR OBEDIENCE

The first blessing focuses on the domestic life of Israel. Every aspect of their agriculture would guarantee everlasting crop production and their villages would prosper. Israel is ADONAI's chosen people; she is the 'pupil of His eye' (Zechariah 2:8). In his commentary, Matthew Henry[73] wrote: *The blessing is promised, upon condition that they diligently hearken to the voice of God. Let them keep up religion, the form and power of it, in their families and nation, then the providence of God would prosper all their outward concerns.*

Unfortunately, as we read throughout the Book of Judges, Israel refused to follow ADONAI's commands and, following the death of Y'hoshua/Joshua, began to worship idols of wood and stone. As Israel forsook the covenant, they were afflicted by attacking nations. Adonai does not allow sins to go unpunished. He will wait until He is ready to impose a judgment.

Throughout these blessings, we see 5 over-arching results[74]: 1. <u>Description of a good man</u> – teachable; sense of need and dependence on others; agreeing to ADONAI's right to instruct and command; reverently listens to ADONAI's voice; open eyes

---

[73] Henry, M., *Matthew Henry's Complete Commentary on the Bible*, <u>Hendrickson Publishers</u>, Volume 1, 2014.

[74] Exell, J.S., Spence-Jones, H., *Commentary of Deuteronomy 28*, <u>The Pulpit Commentary</u>, <u>https://www.studylight.org/commentaries/eng/tpc/deuteronomy-28.html. 1897</u>, accessed 04 October, 2023.

(meaning – generous) and his entire conduct is maintained by the known will of ADONAI. 2. <u>Goodness allied to Greatness</u> – goodness grows into eminence; faithful service crowned with honour. 3. <u>The Reward of Goodness is its own Permanence</u> – individual acts evolve into habits; habits grow in permanence and constitute character. 4. <u>ADONAI may be seen through the blessings given</u> – ADONAI acts through all the natural laws; true prosperity is a gift from ADONAI. 5. <u>A Good Man delights in distributing good</u> – ADONAI works through the good man – *"You will lend to many nations and not borrow"*; all people will see how ADONAI has graced the 'good man'; the good man's influence will spread - *burning and a shining light; many will rejoice in his light.* John 5:35.

THE HEAD, NOT THE TAIL

ADONAI has told Israel they will be a powerful force in the world, if they obey His Word - *When the LORD your God blesses you as He has promised you, you will lend to many nations but not borrow; you will rule over many nations, but they will not rule over you.* Deuteronomy 15:6. God promised Israel power on the world stage.

In Western culture, the saying, 'the tail wagging the dog' connotes an imbalance in the order. This was the case once Israel broke from their commitment to follow ADONAI and began to worship the gods of nations around them. They lost their power and were ruled by other nations until very recently. Only in the 20th Century has Israel begun to see her power being restored. Does this mean Israel is once more following ADONAI? Or does it mean ADONAI'S love continues to pour upon Israel?

GOD'S CURSES

Reading Scripture only may tend to draw people away from the authority of God's Word. Thankfully, there is much historical evidence that supports what Scripture shares with us. The discovery of ancient cuneiform documents, discovered in the 19th Century add credence to the biblical events of I and II Kings, regarding the Assyrian conquest of Israel, 720 BCE, and the Babylonian conquest of Judea, 597 BCE. Granted these are broad strokes of history only and do not go into detail of what happened to the people, but, given how fearsome these warring nations were, it does not take much to realize how difficult these sieges were for the people in Jerusalem.

A reasonable question to ask here is why do ADONAI's curses outnumber His blessings? Thersea Pirola, writing in Light of Torah, suggests *The painful difficulties of life can threaten to eclipse our awareness of God's blessings. How do you live with a fundamental sense of life as gift and blessing? The interpretation above approaches 'curse' as a carefully-applied corrective and presumes that God desires to give people every chance to mend their ways.* [75]

A deeper understanding of blessings and curses is warranted. A blessing is an invitation to be fruitful and multiply and participate in God's life-sustaining power in a secure, abundant environment, whereas a curse is the inverse -- not a vindictive punishment from God. But when humans choose to reject the blessing of life, they automatically choose death.[76]

When ADONAI created order in the universe, He demonstrated His power to bring order from chaos. His blessings to human beings display that power, His strength and might. Curses, then, symbolizes ADONAI's placing humans in the period of time before order was created, meaning those under a curse are relegated to the time of death and destruction before order was brought to chaos.

In the ancient Middle East, nations had created covenants between each other long before Israel was formed as a nation. When two nations entered into a covenant with each other, the blessings indicated what each nation would gain from the treaty; whereas the curses would warn each nation what would happen if either party violated the terms of the covenant.

The covenant referred to in Deuteronomy 28 began in Deuteronomy 27 and are the repeated instructions given in Deuteronomy 11. In Deuteronomy 27, Moshe instructed Israel to divide itself into two groups. One group would advance to Mount Gerizim, where it would pronounce ADONAI's blessings upon Israel, and the other group to Mount Ebal, where this group would pronounce the curses on Israel, if the nation disobeys ADONAI's commands.

The two mountains are near the oaks of Moreh, where Avraham received his first test of faith, as outlined in Genesis 12:1-3 - *Now ADONAI said to Avram, "Get yourself out of your country, away from your kinsmen and away from your father's house, and go to the land that I will show you. I will make of you a great nation, I will bless you, and I will make your name great; and you are to be a blessing. I will bless those who bless you, but I will curse anyone who curses you; and by you all the families of the earth will be blessed."* Connecting the blessings and curses of Deuteronomy 27,28 with Genesis 12, reminds Israel of ADONAI's commitment to

[75] Pirola, T. *Why are there more curses than blessings?*, Light of Torah, 2013, Why Are There More Curses Than Blessings? (lightoftorah.net), accessed 27 June 2024.
[76] Hallo, W. W., *Covenant Curses*, The Bible Project, https://bibleproject.com/podcast/covenant-curses/#:~:text=In%20this%20last%20movement%20of,ancient%20Near%20Eastern%20law%20treaties. Accessed 06 October, 2023.

their patriarchs. In addition, there is an implicit recognition of ADONAI's blessings of Eden on human beings, who continued to follow His commands.

FINAL NATURAL BLESSINGS

The natural blessings, written in Chapter 29, focus on how ADONAI cared for and protected His people, as they wandered through the wilderness for 40 years. During this period of time, the first generation of Israel, those who had rebelled against and rejected ADONAI's Word 10 times, died and were replaced by the second generation, those who appeared to be obedient to ADONAI. The enumeration of these blessings is introduced with a rather strange pronouncement. Moshe said to Israel, *Yet to this day the LORD has not given you a mind to understand, eyes to see, or ears to hear.* Deuteronomy 29:4.

John Piper[77], at the Gospel Coalition Women's Conference, June 16, 2018, called this statement 'The Impossible Covenant'. By this he meant 'If your heart turns to God as your supreme Treasure, God has turned your heart back', First Kings 18:27: *"Answer me, O Lord, answer me, that this people may know that you, O Lord, are God, and that you have turned their hearts back."* That's what Elijah wanted them, and the men of Israel, to know: If human hearts turn back to God, God has turned them back. This is what it means for God to be God. And therefore He aims to be known and loved and treasured as God." In other words, in order for people to see ADONAI as their supreme Sovereign, the Ruler of the universe and their true treasure, their hearts must be turned towards ADONAI. Humans cannot achieve this on their own.

Even though they have seen and have been told of the marvels and wonders ADONAI had produced with and for Israel, they did not really understand that He had produced these. They did not comprehend the depth of these marvels, such as their clothes lasting 40 years without wear, violated God's own laws of nature. What did they not see? They did not understand that ADONAI was their supreme Treasure, their precious Treasure. They had seen Him as powerful but not as precious. It appears their earthly needs seemed to have dulled their hearts to ADONAI'S signs and wonders.

This is the completion of our seventh weekly reading.

May the God of Abraham, Isaac and Jacob bless you fully and richly.

---

[77] John Piper is a theologian, author, pastor and chancellor of Bethlehem College and Seminary, Minneapolis, Minnesota.

PARASHAH NITZAVIM (STANDING)

DEUTERONOMY 29:10 TO 30:20

THIS OUR EIGHTH WEEKLY READING OF SEFER D'VARIM, THE BOOK OF DEUTERONOMY. THIS IS MOSHE'S FINAL DAY OF LIFE AND THIS IS THE LAST TIME HE WILL HAVE TO IMPART HIS THOUGHTS AND TEACHINGS TO ISRAEL. THESE LAST TEACHINGS INTRODUCE TO THE PEOPLE THE PRINCIPAL OF RESPONSIBILITY FOR ONE ANOTHER. EACH ISRAELITE IS RESPONSIBLE TO ASSIST HER/HIS NEIGHBOUR TO OBSERVE TORAH AND RESTRAIN FROM VIOLATING IT.

PLEASE READ THE PASSAGE FOCUSED ON HERE BEFORE YOU ENGAGE THE TEXT.

Parashah Nitzavim (Standing)

Deuteronomy 29:10 to 30:20

*All of you are standing today before the L*ORD *your God—your leaders, tribes, elders, officials, all the men of Israel, your children, your wives, and the foreigners in your camps who cut your wood and draw your water— so that you may enter into the covenant of the L*ORD *your God, which He is making with you today, so that you may enter into His oath and so that He may establish you today as His people and He may be your God as He promised you and as He swore to your fathers Abraham, Isaac, and Jacob. I am making this covenant and this oath not only with you, but also with those who are standing here with us today in the presence of the L*ORD *our God and with those who are not here today.*

Deuteronomy 29:10-15

The beginning of this week's reading reiterates the covenant ADONAI has made with Israel, just before they crossed the Yarden/Jordan River. Notice the covenant extends far beyond the boundaries of time even to this present age, as we read in verse 15 - *and with those who are not here today.*

Verses 16 to 21 focus on Moshe's concern that Israelites will abandon the covenant made with ADONAI and with him. Let's read a portion of this message: *When someone hears the words of this oath, he may consider himself exempt, thinking, 'I will have peace even though I follow my own stubborn heart.' This will lead to the destruction of the well-watered land as well as the dry land.* Deuteronomy 29:19. Another version, the Complete Jewish Bible, presents verse 19 as: *If there is such a person, when he hears the words of this curse, he will bless himself secretly, saying to himself, 'I will be all right, even though I will stubbornly keep doing whatever I feel like doing; so that I, although "dry," [sinful,] will be added to the "watered" [righteous]'* Deuteronomy 29:19 CJB. It should be noted that ADONAI has even declared the land would suffer, because of Israel's malfeasance. Indeed, ADONAI would not be able to accept Israel's turning away from Him, inflicting upon His people all the curses written in Torah.

With this punishment upon Israel, other nations will observe that ADONAI's anger will be vicious as it descended upon Israel. A short portion will exemplify His anger: *They began to worship other gods, bowing down to gods they had not known—gods that the LORD had not permitted them to worship. Therefore, the LORD's anger burned against this land, and He brought every curse written in this book on it. The LORD uprooted them from their land in His anger, rage, and great wrath, and threw them into another land where they are today.* Deuteronomy 29:26-28.

The final words of Chapter 29, speak to the lasting impact of history in the lives of Jewish people - *The hidden things belong to the LORD our God, but the revealed things belong to us and our children forever, so that we may follow all the words of this law.* Deuteronomy 29:29.

The second and final chapter of this week's reading, Chapter 30, begins with the ways Israel may ask ADONAI to repair the rift between them. Here is a short portion: *When all these things happen to you—the blessings and curses I have set before you—and you come to your senses while you are in all the nations where the LORD your God has driven you, and you and your children return to the LORD your God and obey Him with all your heart and all your soul by doing everything I am giving you today, then He will restore your fortunes, have compassion on you, and gather you again from all the peoples where the LORD your God has scattered you. Even if your exiles are at the ends of the earth, He will gather you and bring you back from there.* Deuteronomy 30:1-4. Indeed, ADONAI promises to restore all of Israel's former glories as His nation when they return to worship Him and follow His teachings. Verse 10 displays His compassion on them: *when you obey the LORD your God by keeping His commands and statutes that are written in this book of the law and return to Him with all your heart and all your soul.*

Verses 11 to 20, of Deuteronomy 30, help Israel understand that ADONAI's teaching is not difficult to find; indeed, it is with Israel constantly. Let's read a portion of this teaching: *This command that I give you today is certainly not too difficult or beyond your reach. It is not in heaven so that you have to ask, 'Who will go up to heaven, get it for us, and proclaim it to us so that we may follow it?' And it is not across the sea so that you have to ask, 'Who will cross the sea, get it for us, and proclaim it to us so that we may follow it?' But the message is very near you, in your mouth and in your heart, so that you may follow it.* Deuteronomy 30:11-14.

The final two verses of Chapter 30 provide a closing to this message. Let's look at these verses: *I call heaven and earth as witnesses against you today that I have set before you life and death, blessing and curse. Choose life so that you and your descendants may live, love the LORD your God, obey Him, and remain faithful to Him. For He is your life, and He will prolong your life in the land the LORD swore to give to your fathers Abraham, Isaac, and Jacob.* Deuteronomy 30:19,20. These two verses indicate the purpose Adonai has for Israel – loving Adonai and being faithful to His commands. This, then, creates the purpose of the lives of Israel's people.

This concludes our eighth weekly reading of Hasefer
D'Varim, the Book of Deuteronomy.

DEEPER UNDERSTANDINGS

ADONAI'S COVENANT

This is not an unusual covenant ADONAI originally made with Israel. Moshe reiterated ADONAI's covenant made with Avraham, as we read in Genesis 15. A short portion of the passage will be appropriate: *When the sun had set and it was dark, a smoking fire pot and a flaming torch appeared and passed between the divided animals. On that day the LORD made a covenant with Abram, saying, "I give this land to your offspring, from the brook of Egypt to the Euphrates River: the land of the Kenites, Kenizzites, Kadmonites, Hittites, Perizzites, Rephaim, Amorites, Canaanites, Girgashites, and Jebusites."* Genesis 15:17-21.

As has been noted, the covenant was intended not only for those standing before Moshe that day but also for all those who were to come. That includes all who are natural and spiritual Israel today.

ABANDONING THE COVENANT

As Moshe had warned a few times in Sefer HaD'Varim, the Book of Deuteronomy, there would be a huge cost to Israel, if they abandoned any of the covenants ADONAI made with them. In this respect, he is behaving in his role as a prophet, whose purpose was to prepare people for what was to happen, given their life choices.

Moshe functioned through a three-fold ministry – prophet, priest and king (leader). These roles foreshadowed the three-fold ministry of ADONAI YESHUA, who also functioned and will function as prophet, priest and king, when He returns.

As history has shown, when Israel did turn away from ADONAI and followed their own course, they were removed from the land at great cost in lives and future. ADONAI Elohim often uses people to complete His promises, good and bad. The ten northern tribes living in the land of Dan were uprooted by the Assyrians in 722 BCE, following a 3-year siege by the Emperor Shalmaneser V.

Insert in a dialogue box. During the 20th Century, before Hitler came to power in Germany, the Jewish people were in positions of prominence. The desire of many was to assimilate into the German community and be as one with their neighbours. Many forsook their Jewish practices and their love for ADONAI. Could this be one reason for the Holocaust?

REPAIRING THE RIFT

Whenever ADONAI curses an individual or a nation for their sinful behaviour, He provides a way out of the curse. In 1 Corinthians 10:13 Rav Sha'ul, the Apostle Paul, shares with us: *No temptation has overtaken you except what is common to humanity. God is faithful, and He will not allow you to be tempted beyond what you are able, but with the temptation He will also provide a way of escape so that you are able to bear it.* This tells us clearly that we have an escape available for us if we desire to use it. For Israel, as we read in Deuteronomy 30, the escape from the curse that will be imposed upon them is their return to Torah and ADONAI's life lesson teaching. In all cases, with Israel and with all peoples, the inescapable process is no different – *'teshuvah'*, repentance, asking for forgiveness and renouncing sinful behaviour, is required.

Israel's Message

At the time of Moshe, Israel had only one written scroll of his teaching. As a result, they were taught by their leaders and their fathers. Every child was taught to memorize the words shared with them, from the prophets and from Torah. By the time they were twelve or thirteen, every male child was expected to have a fundamental understanding of Hasefer D'Varim, the Book of Deuteronomy.

As we read in Exodus 19:6, Adonai selected Israel to be His priests for the world: *you will be my kingdom of priests and my holy nation.* However, when they rebelled against Adonai and Moshe, as we find in Exodus 32, with the creation of the golden calf, Israel was found to be inadequate to hold that position. The only tribe that stood with Moshe were the Levites; they were selected to be Israel's priests, as we read in Numbers 3:5-9.

Those who were trained to be Levitical priests and workers in the Tabernacle, received much more training, as might be assumed, as their duties included: the teaching of the Law, Leviticus 10:11; offering the sacrifices, Leviticus chapter 9; maintaining the Tabernacle and the Temple, Numbers 18:3; officiating in the Holy Place, Exodus 30:7-10; inspecting ceremonially unclean persons, Leviticus chapters 13 and 14; they adjudicated disputes, Deuteronomy 17:8-13; they functioned as tax collectors, Numbers 18:21,26; Hebrews 7:5.[78] Specific teachers and leaders from within the Levitical ranks would be tasked with teaching the children, who would memorize all the Torah perfectly, before they reached their age to assume duties within the Tabernacle.

[78] Robertson, R., *The Jewish Question in German Literature, 1749-1939*, Oxford University Press, Pp. 233-378, October 2001, Oxford, U.K.
[64] *Grace Notes*, Austin Bible Church, Austin Texas, 2017. https://www2.gracenotes.info/topics/levitical-priesthood.html, accessed 02 November, 2023.

REMAINING FAITHFUL

As has been mentioned earlier, every verb in Hebrew has an action associated with it. Thus, the command, *remain faithful to Him*, may be read, 'follow His commands and do not stray from His teachings'. The literal understanding of this phrase might be, 'hold on to Him' (Deuteronomy 10:20), meaning to keep following and do not wander away from Him.

This concludes our eighth Weekly Reading.

PARASHAH VAYELEKH – HE WENT

DEUTERONOMY 31:1-30

IN THIS, OUR NINTH READING OF SEFER D'VARIM, WE WITNESS MOSHE VISITING EACH OF THE TRIBES AND BIDDING THEM FAREWELL. HE WISHED TO CONSOLE THEM OVER HIS IMPENDING DEATH. HE DID NOT WANT THEIR SADNESS TO DARKEN THEIR JOY OF HAVING SEALED THE COVENANT.

PLEASE READ THE PASSAGE FOCUSED ON HERE BEFORE YOU ENGAGE THE TEXT.

PARASHAH VAYELEKH – HE WENT

DEUTERONOMY 31:1-30

Then Moses continued to speak these words to all Israel, saying,
"I am now 120 years old; I can no longer act as your leader.
The LORD has told me, 'You will not cross this Jordan.'

Deuteronomy 31:1,2.

Moshe's first words to each of the tribes of Israel were designed to reassure them that ADONAI would lead them further and take them across the Jordan River into the promised land. Their hopes and dreams would finally come to fruition. Here are Moshe's words - *The LORD your God is the One who will cross ahead of you. He will destroy these nations before you, and you will drive them out. Joshua is the one who will cross ahead of you, as the LORD has said.* In these two sentences Moshe assures his people that ADONAI will be their protector and leader and that they will be humanly led by Y'hoshua, who has been with them for the past 40 years, as Moshe's 'right-hand' man. The final statement in his short talk with each of the tribes, *For it is the LORD your God who goes with you; He will not leave you or forsake you,* was designed to fully settle them in the understanding ADONAI was their Leader, their King.

Having visited all the tribes, Moshe then spoke with Y'hoshua, before all the people, and encouraged him in his new task. Let's read that statement: *Be strong and courageous, for you will go with this people into the land the LORD swore to give to their fathers. You will enable them to take possession of it. The LORD is the One who will go before you. He will be with you; He will not leave you or forsake you. Do not be afraid or discouraged.* Deuteronomy 31:7,8. As well as encouraging Y'hoshua in his new role, Moshe is telling him that he will be the one causing Israel to inherit their land.

As his final task, Moshe completed transcribing what he had been teaching Israel in this Book, the Book of Deuteronomy, and presented it to the Levites. They were now responsible for the teaching of Israel, as we read in Deuteronomy 31:26 His words are very important here: *At the end of every seven years, at the appointed time in the year of debt cancellation, during the Festival of Booths, when all Israel assembles in the presence of the LORD your God at the place He chooses, you are to read this law aloud before all Israel. Gather the people—men, women, children, and foreigners living within your gates—so that they may listen and learn to fear the LORD your God and be careful to follow all the words of this law. Then their children who do not know the law will listen and learn to fear the LORD your God as long as you live in the land you are crossing the Jordan to possess.* Deuteronomy 31:10-13.

Verses 14 and 15 begin the process of Y'hoshua's commissioning, as the new leader of Israel. We read of the actual ceremony in verse 23: *The LORD commissioned Joshua son of Nun, "Be strong and courageous, for you will bring the Israelites into the land I swore to them, and I will be with you."*

The final task ADONAI gave Moshe was the transcribing of His song that Moshe was to teach Israel. We will read this song in our next chapter of Deuteronomy. Israel's task was to recite it until they had it memorized, for as ADONAI said, *And when many troubles and afflictions come to them, this song will testify against them, because their descendants will not have forgotten it.*

Finally, Moshe gathered the Levites and presented them with his final written version of Sefer D'Varim, the Book of Deuteronomy, a papyrus scroll, to be used to teach Israel. He then shared his personal feelings with Israel about their future. One of these verses will help us understand his concerns: *For I know that after my death you will become completely corrupt and turn from the path I have commanded you. Disaster will come to you in the future because you will do what is evil in the LORD's sight, infuriating Him with what your hands have made.* Deuteronomy 31:29.

Moshe's final task was to teach Israel the song ADONAI commanded him to transcribe. We will meet this song in our next weekly reading.

This is the end of our ninth weekly reading of Hasefer
D'Varim, the Book of Deuteronomy.

Deeper Understandings

The Shemitah

The *Shemitah* (Sh'mittah) was held on the seventh year after Israel entered the holy land and from then on. During this holy time, all debts were to be cancelled and Hebrew slaves were offered their freedom, with a small endowment, enabling them to begin a new life. We find this command presented in Exodus 21, 23; Leviticus 25; and Deuteronomy 15.

The Book Moshe Transcribed

There has been much speculation about the 'book' Moshe transcribed to be presented to Israel. First, this was not a codex, or book with pages we turn. Rather, this was a papyrus scroll, written by hand. The codex was not invented before the end of the first century CE. Now as to what scroll was created, let's explore this.

Jean-Pierre Sonnet, writing in The Book within the Book[79], claims that Moshe wrote "the comprehensive Torah 'book'." Jeffery Tigay, writing in his article, JPS Torah Commentary: Deuteronomy[80], asserts Moshe only transcribed the Book of Deuteronomy. However, as Moshe did not specify what portion of Torah he transcribed, it will be next to impossible to be absolute in a declaration.

This completes the ninth Weekly Reading.

May you be fully and richly blessed by the God of Abraham, Isaac and Jacob.

---

[79] Sonnet, J.P., *The Book within the Book*, Leiden, E.J. Brill, 1997, p. 166.
[80] Tigay, J., *JPS Torah Commentary: Deuteronomy*, JPS Torah Commentary, The Jewish Publication Society, Philadelphia, 1996, p. 297.

Parashah Ha'azinu – Hear

Deuteronomy 32:1-52

In this song, ADONAI taught Moshe, we read of heaven and earth being called to bear witness to what Israel will need to undergo, when it sins against ADONAI. The song concludes with the ultimate joy of redemption, when Israel returns to her Most Holy God.

Please read the passage focused on here before you engage the text.

Parashah Ha'azinu – Hear

Deuteronomy 32:1-52

Hear, oh heavens, as I speak! Listen, earth, to the words from my mouth!
May my teaching fall like rain. May my speech condense like dew,
like light rain on blades of grass, or showers on growing plants.

Deuteronomy 32:1,2

The two final chapters of HaSefer D'Varim/the Book of Deuteronomy and Torah is only one chapter in length. Chapter 32 presents us with the Song of Moshe, in which Moshe appeals to heaven and earth to be witnesses to the curses which will come upon Israel, when, as a nation she sins against ADONAI's commands and the great joy which will fall upon Israel with her final redemption.

The first 4 verses set the scene for us and urges Israel to listen carefully to Moshe's teaching. Read a passage with me: *Pay attention, heavens, and I will speak; listen, earth, to the words of my mouth. Let my teaching fall like rain and my word settle like dew, like gentle rain on new grass and showers on tender plants. For I will proclaim Yahweh's name. Declare the greatness of our God!* Deuteronomy 32:1-3. Moshe asked all of creation to listen to his song, the words of which are tender as dew dropping on flowers and leaves of the fields. The final verse, verse 4 of this introduction, praises the power and glory of ADONAI. Read this with me: *The Rock -- His work is perfect; all His ways are entirely just. A faithful God, without prejudice, He is righteous and true.*

The next section, verses 5 – 9, chastises Israel for his disobedience and rebellion against his God. He, Moshe, then reminds Israel of the love ADONAI showered them and claiming that they are His people. Here is a portion: *His people have acted corruptly toward Him; this is their defect -- they are not His children but a devious and crooked generation . . . Remember the days of old; consider the years long past.*

Ask your father, and he will tell you, your elders, and they will teach you . . . But the Lord's portion is His people, Jacob, His own inheritance. Deuteronomy 32:5, 7, 9.

Verses 10 – 14 reminded Israel of ADONAI's caring for His children, bringing them out of *a desolate land, in a barren, howling wilderness* (Deuteronomy 32:10), and protecting them, as the apple of His eye, as *an eagle and hovers over His young; He spreads His wings, catches him, and lifts him up on His pinions.* Deuteronomy 32:11. These are comforting verses for Israel, as they prepare to cross the Yarden River and begin expelling Cana'anites from the lands Israel will occupy.

In verses 15 to 18, Moshe recounts how Israel rebelled against ADONAI and turned from His path. Let's read a portion: *They provoked His jealousy with foreign gods; they enraged Him with detestable practices. They sacrificed to demons, not God, to gods they had not known, new gods that had just arrived, which your fathers did not fear.* Deuteronomy 32:16,17.

Through verses 19 to 22, Moshe recounts ADONAI's anger against Israel's rebellious behaviour. The extend of His anger may be seen in verse 22: *For fire has been kindled because of My anger and burns to the depths of Sheol; it devours the land and its produce, and scorches the foundations of the mountains.*

How ADONAI's anger was translated into action may be evidenced in verses 23 to 25. Here is a portion: *I will pile disasters on them; I will use up My arrows against them. They will be weak from hunger, ravaged by pestilence and bitter plague; I will unleash on them wild beasts with fangs, as well as venomous snakes that slither in the dust.* Deuteronomy 32:23,24.

ADONAI's anger may have extended into Israel's destruction, if it wouldn't have been for the reaction of warring nations around them. Because of His caution, His actions were somewhat reserved. We may read this in the following segment: *I would have said: I will cut them to pieces and blot out the memory of them from mankind, if I had not feared insult from the enemy, or feared that these foes might misunderstand and say: 'Our own hand has prevailed; it wasn't the Lord who did all this'.* Deuteronomy 32:26,27.

In verses 26 to 33, Moshe recounts ADONAI's perception of Israel's lack of wisdom and discernment. All they had to do was analyze what was happening to them to see the consequences of their rebellion, as we may see in the following: *Israel is a nation lacking sense with no understanding at all. If only they were wise, they would figure it out; they would understand their fate. How could one man pursue a thousand, or two put ten thousand to flight, unless their Rock had sold them, unless the Lord had given them up?* Deuteronomy 32:28 – 30. However, analyzing behaviour is not as simple as it seems. Israel lacked wisdom and discernment, as a result, they did not have *the power to see and the inclination to choose.* Proverbs 9.

The next section of the Song, verses 34 to 42, reveal ADONAI's plans for vengeance against Israel, for her rebellion and idolatry. The following passage demonstrates a portion of this plan: *Is it not stored up with Me, sealed up in My vaults? Vengeance belongs to Me; I will repay. In time their foot will slip, for their day of disaster is near, and their doom is coming quickly.* Deuteronomy 32:34,35.

The final verse of the Song of Moshe, verse 43, ends on a positive note, sharing ADONAI's love for Israel and His desire to see Israel's enemy's defeated. Let's read that verse: *Rejoice, you nations, concerning His people, for He will avenge the blood of His servants. He will take vengeance on His adversaries; He will purify His land and His people.*

Moshe, accompanied by Y'hoshua, his replacement, recited the Song to Israel, as they waited on the shoreline of the Yarden River. In sharing the Song with Israel, Moshe assured them that ADONAI's words were true and that His promises would come to pass, should Israel stray off His path. Here is an except: *For they are not meaningless words to you but they are your life, and by them you will live long in the land you are crossing the Jordan to possess.* Deuteronomy 32:47.

In the final 5 verses of this week's parashah, Moshe recounts ADONAI's words to him, reminding him of ADONAI's promise to bring Moshe to his death on Mount Nebo. A short segment of this section will demonstrate His promise and the reason: *For both of you broke faith with Me among the Israelites at the waters of Meribath-kadesh in the Wilderness of Zin by failing to treat Me as holy in their presence. Although from a distance you will view the land that I am giving the Israelites, you will not go there.* Deuteronomy 32:51,52.

This ends our tenth Weekly Reading of HaSefer
D'Varim, the Book of Deuteronomy.

DEEPER UNDERSTANDINGS

BROAD OVERVIEW OF THE SONG OF MOSHE

If portions of the Song of Moshe seem harsh, it was intended as a clear wake-up call to Israel to alert them to the fact that, in the future, their behaviour will bring much anger to their God and cause Him to discipline them severely for that behaviour. And, indeed, that is what happened. As we read in the prophets

(Jonah 790 – 770 BCE; Joel 790 – 770 BCE; Amos 780 – 740 BCE; Hosea 760 – 720 BCE; Isaiah 745 – 695 BCE; Micah 740 – 700 BCE; Zephaniah 639 – 608 BCE and Nachum 630 – 608 BCE) ADONAI's justice and punishment was brought against both Israel for their rebellion against their Father and against Assyria, the weapon used by ADONAI to bring about His judgment.

In the Song we also see contrasted the perfect quality of ADONAI's character with the very low character of Israel's future behaviour. The perfect nature of ADONAI's character is demonstrated in the litany of blessings He has bestowed upon Israel. This is held in contrast to the ill-will Israel has shown to their God.

ADONAI's future judgment for their rebellion is demonstrated in the verses which describe the wars which will befall Israel, once they were settled in their land and have begun to commit adultery, with other gods and idols. This is followed by ADONAI's promise to destroy Israel's enemies and to bring redemption to the remnant of Israel that will be left.

The Song ends with Moshe exhorting Israel to keep the words and understandings of the Song in their hearts, although we read in the Prophets, they were rarely heeded.

Chapter 32 ends with ADONAI commanding Moshe to climb to the summit of Mount Nebo, which is currently in the State of Jordan.

MEANING OF THE SONG TODAY

Many people have expressed difficulty in believing the Word of ADONAI issued in the days of Moshe would have relevance today. However, as every serious student of His Word knows, the vast majority of the prophecies contained in the Old Covenant have come to pass. This is particularly true of the prophecies relating to ADONAI YESHUA, the LORD JESUS. However, what is often more difficult to understand is the reality that ancient prophecies often have two or more layers of meaning – one for the immediate time period and others for future times.

Throughout the history of Israel, as a people not as a state, many calamities have befallen them, when they turned from their calling as *My kingdom of priests and My holy nation.* Exodus 19:6. As His priests, Israel was to teach the world how to follow Torah, ADONAI's life instructions, and help other nations to maintain holy lives. This promise followed an earlier one, in which ADONAI avowed that through Avraham *all the peoples on earth will be blessed through you.*

As history informs us, each time His people strayed from following Him, they were disciplined. Through the prophets, we have seen that Israel, the 10 northern tribes, endured the exile imposed by the Assyrian Empire, in 720 BCE. Then, in 597 BCE, the 2 southern tribes of Y'hudah, Judah, were captured by the Babylonian Empire and exiled for 70 years.

Israel endured other exiles as well; for example, in 130 CE, the Roman Empire destroyed Jerusalem and many little towns around the city and forced hundreds of thousands of Judeans into slavery, while at least one million were killed. We do know that believers received word from ADONAI YESHUA, the LORD JESUS, prior to this event, when He said, as recorded in Matthew 24:15,16 - *So when you see the abomination that causes devastation spoken about through the prophet Dani'el standing in the Holy Place" (let the reader understand the allusion), that will be the time for those in Y'hudah to escape to the hills,* many did flee the city. Those few who were left had great enmity for believers who fled to places like Petra, and avoided the slaughter of the Roman legions. That enmity exists today.

All through the history of Europe, we read about Jews being persecuted from one country to another. In Spain, for example, Jews were ordered out of the country by Ferdinand and Isabella, in 1492.

In later years, similar atrocities occurred that caused the extermination of millions of Jewish people. The Holocaust (1941-1945), for example, reduced the Jewish population in Europe by 6 million, almost 2/3 of the population[81]. In addition the Nazis also killed 5 million other people, including Roma (Gypsies), Blacks, homosexuals and other minorities, such as those with disabilities and Jehovah's Witnesses, believed to be inferior to the aryian race. In Europe, during the early to mid 20th Century, Jewish people desired to assimilate with European culture and tended to abandon their traditional worship of ADONAI, although they often continued their cultural traditions[82].

Today, as I write this, antisemitism is on the rise, especially among radical groups, such as white supremacists and other holocaust deniers. The current movement appears

[81] Holocaust Encyclopedia, European Jewish Population Distribution, CA, 1933, 1950, Holocaust Encyclopedia, http://www.encyclopedia.ushmm.org., accessed 31 March, 2024.
[82] Robertson, R., Ibid., Pp. 233-378.

to be growing in strength in the United States, Britain, Germany, France, South Africa and countries in South America[83]. Canada has also experienced an increase in antisemitic activity, especially in Toronto and Montreal.

For a clearer understanding of what is coming, I recommend you read the Book of Revelation, a truly Jewish prophecy of the coming end days.

This concludes our tenth Weekly Reading.
May the God of Abraham, Isaac and Jacob bless you fully and richly.

---

[83] McAskill, A. et.al., *How the surge in antisemitism is affecting countries around the world*, <u>Reuters</u>, October 31, 2023.

Parashah V'Zot HaBrachah

This is the Blessing
Deuteronomy 33:1 to 34:12

This is the eleventh and final Parashah of torah. Here Moshe blesses each of the tribes of Israel before they enter the promised land. This appears to be a continuation of Ya'akov's (Jacob) blessings of his sons, before his death.

Please read the passage focused on here before you engage the text.

Parashah V'Zot HaBrachah

This is the Blessing
Deuteronomy 33:1 to 34:12

The blessings Moshe shared with the 12 tribes of Israel were a combination of blessings and prophecies, prior to his death and to Israel's crossing the River Yarden (Jordan River). As we read these blessings for each tribe, we may see the prophecy included.

The introduction to the chapter is interesting. Here the narrator tells us: *This is the blessing that Moses, the man of God, gave the Israelites before his death.* Deuteronomy 33:1. The phrase, *the man of God*, indicates Moshe's status as being able to speak on behalf of ADONAI. How ADONAI loved His chosen disciple.

The first 6 verses of the Parashah speak to ADONAI's love for Israel. Let's read a portion: *The LORD came from Sinai and appeared to them from Seir; He shone on them from Mount Paran and came with ten thousand holy ones, with lightning from His right hand for them. Indeed He loves the people. All Your holy ones are in Your hand, and they assemble at Your feet. Each receives Your words.*
Deuteronomy 33:1-3.

Verse 6 presents an interesting interjection to the blessings: *Let Reuben live and not die though his people become few.* There are two possible explanations for this 'blessing'. Rashi[84] claims that Reuben carried the tribe's namesake curse for having violated the bed of Bilhah, as we read in Genesis 35. However, a more pertinent rational is that Reuben was the first tribe to receive its ancestral heritage, on the east bank of the Yarden River, as we read in Deuteronomy 33:5. The reality of Reuben being the largest tribe of Israel and the firstborn son of Ya'akov, might help in understanding the tribe being selected first.

The blessing for Y'hudah is rather short: *LORD, hear Judah's cry and bring him to*

---

[84] Shlomo Yitzchaki, Rashi, a medieval French rabbi who wrote numerous commentaries of Talmud and Torah. He lived between 1040 and 1105 CE.

his people. He fights for his cause with his own hands, but may You be a help against his foes. Deuteronomy 33:7.

Let's read a portion of Moshe's blessing for the tribe of Levi: *Your Thummim and Urim belong to Your faithful one; You tested him at Massah and contended with him at the waters of Meribah. He said about his father and mother, "I do not regard them." He disregarded his brothers and didn't acknowledge his sons, for they kept Your word and maintained Your covenant.* Deuteronomy 33:8,9. As you read through the complete blessing, you may notice the love for Levi that Moshe expresses.

The blessing Moshe gave Binyamine was very short:

The LORD's beloved rests securely on Him. He shields him all day long, and he rests on His shoulders.

We clearly see the youngest son of Ya'akov, Jacob, was ADONAI's beloved.

Joseph's blessing carries with it the theme of favour being given to the two tribes of Ephraim and Manasseh. Let's read a short passage:

May these rest on the head of Joseph, on the crown of the prince of his brothers. His firstborn bull has splendor, and horns like those of a wild ox; he gores all the peoples with them to the ends of the earth. Such are the ten thousands of Ephraim, and such are the thousands of Manasseh. Deuteronomy 33:16b, 17.

Notice that Moshe blesses Zebulun and Issachar together. This maybe due to the fact that the brothers came from the same mother and were together much of their lives. This issue is discussed below, in Deeper Understandings. Here is Moshe's blessing of the two tribes:

Rejoice, Zebulun, in your journeys, and Issachar, in your tents. They summon the peoples to a mountain; there they offer acceptable sacrifices. For they draw from the wealth of the seas and the hidden treasures of the sand.

Deuteronomy 33:18,19.

The line, *They summon the peoples to a mountain,* refers to the nations who trade for fish with these tribes, living on the shores of the Sea of Galilee. These are gentile nations who will be brought to Israel to worship the True God once the Temple is constructed.

The blessing Moshe gave to the tribe of Gad had a prophetic ring to it. A part of verse 20 states, *He lies down like a lion and tears off an arm or even a head;* this section of the verse indicates Gad's role in the conquest of the promised land, when Israel began its invasion. These were fierce fighters and they aided greatly in conquering the land. Then, in the final portion of verse 21 we read: *he carried out the LORD's justice and His ordinances for Israel.* One of the commentators of The Bible Says[85] described the prophetic aspect of the blessing as, *The Gadites fulfilled their obligation and were thus praised for their commitment to the covenantal laws of God. They indeed executed righteousness and lived according to God's precepts in their land.*

The blessing over Dan is very short and not all that complementary: *He said about Dan: Dan is a young lion, leaping out of Bashan.* Deuteronomy 33:22. As we have learned, Dan was an aggressive tribe. This characteristic was evident in Judges 18, where we read of Dan moving from their assigned inheritance of the western coast to the north. When they arrived they slaughtered all the people who inhabited this region. It is speculated they did not trust ADONAI to support them when they attempted to conquer their territory. When they desired to assume the territory occupied by the Philistines, they found them to be a fierce fighting group and decide to abandon the land assigned them.

Dan eventually settled north of the Galilee, including the area known as
Bashan. This is a rich and fertile area of the nation and is now known as the Golan Heights. As we know, this has been disputed territory, since Israel was granted the territory in 1917, through the Balfour Declaration.[86]

Moshe's blessing of Naphtali contains more favourable language than that of Dan: *Naphtali, enjoying approval, full of the LORD's blessing, take possession to the west and the south.* Deuteronomy 33:23.

Finally, in the blessing over Asher, Moshe's words are sweet and very positive. Here is a sample: *May Asher be the most blessed of the sons; may he be the most favored among his brothers and dip his foot in olive oil.* Deuteronomy 33:24. Here we see again the prophetic nature of Moshe's blessings. Asher, meaning fortunate, was to be materially more wealthy than the other tribes. Their land was rich in olive orchards and they prospered more than the other tribes, because of their natural wealth. Given their territory had access to the Mediterranean Ocean, Asher was also more vulnerable to attack than were the other tribes. Thus, Moshe's blessing also called for their tribal gates to be blocked *with bolts of your gate be iron and bronze, and your strength last as long as you live.* Deuteronomy 33:25.

In verses 26 and 27, Moshe recognizes the power of ADONAI, asserting that all blessings come from directly from him: *who rides the heavens to your aid, the*

---

[85] *Deuteronomy 20 – 21 Meaning*, <u>The Bible Says</u>, https://thebiblesays.com/commentary/deut/deut-33/deuteronomy-3320-1/#:~:text=This%20means%20that%20Gad%20occupied,and%20His%20ordinances%20with%20Israel. Accessed 27 December, 2023.

[86] Arthur James Balfour, 1848 to 1930, Earl of Balfour, Prime Minister of B'ritain 1902-1905, first Lord of the Admiralty 1915 to 1916; foreign secretary to Llyod George, 1916 to 1919.

clouds in His majesty. The God of old is your dwelling place, and underneath are the everlasting arms. Deuteronomy 33:26,27. Here we begin the conclusion of his message to the tribes.

The next section of the chapter deals with Israel's security in their new land: *So Israel dwells securely; Jacob lives untroubled in a land of grain and new wine; even his skies drip with dew.* Deuteronomy 33:28. Finally, Moshe speaks of ADONAI's blessings on Israel as a nation, as we see in this verse: *He is the shield that protects you, the sword you boast in. Your enemies will cringe before you, and you will tread on their backs.* Deuteronomy 33:29.

In the last chapter of Deuteronomy, Chapter 34, ADONAI gives Moshe a visual tour of the holy land, the land He had promised to Avraham, Yitzchak and Ya'akov. Let's read a portion of this tour: *the LORD showed him all the land: Gilead as far as Dan, all of Naphtali, the land of Ephraim and Manasseh, all the land of Judah as far as the Mediterranean Sea, the Negev, and the region from the Valley of Jericho, the City of Palms, as far as Zoar. The LORD then said to him, "This is the land I promised Abraham, Isaac, and Jacob, 'I will give it to your descendants.' I have let you see it with your own eyes, but you will not cross into it."* Deuteronomy 34:1-4.

We are given a good deal of information in verses 5 to 8. First, we learn that Moshe died in the valley of Moav/Moab, which is just by the Yarden River, just east of the Dead Sea in what is now west-central Jordan: *So Moses the servant of the LORD died there in the land of Moab, as the LORD had said.* Deuteronomy 34:5. Then, we are told ADONAI buried His servant in a place which would never be discovered: *He buried him in the valley in the land of Moab facing Beth-peor, and no one to this day knows where his grave is.* Deuteronomy 34:6. The narrator shares with us Moshe's age as being 120 years. Despite his age, ADONAI's servant was still vigorous and full of vitality: *Moses was 120 years old when he died; his eyes were not weak, and his vitality had not left him.* Deuteronomy 34:7. Finally, we learn the official mourning for a leader of Israel was 30 days, at that time: *The Israelites wept for Moses in the plains of Moab 30 days.* Deuteronomy 34:8a.

The first part of the last paragraph shares with us the new leader of Israel, Y'hoshua/Joshua, was filled with wisdom, as Moshe had laid hands of him, transferring ADONAI's power: *Joshua son of Nun was filled with the spirit of wisdom because Moses had laid his hands on him. So the Israelites obeyed him and did as the LORD had commanded Moses.* Deuteronomy 34:9.

The final portion of Sefer HaD'Varim, the Book of Deuteronomy, shares with us how ADONAI blessed Moshe and gifted him with His rank of greatest prophet: *No prophet has arisen again in Israel like Moses, whom the Lord knew face to face.* Deuteronomy 34:10. Then ADONAI's great works through Moshe are shared with us: *He was unparalleled for all the signs and wonders the Lord sent him to do against the land of Egypt—to Pharaoh, to all his officials, and to all his land, and for all the mighty acts of power and terrifying deeds that Moses performed in the sight of all Israel.* Deuteronomy 34:11,12.

This ends our final reading of Torah.

May the God of Avraham, Yitzchak and Ya'akov bless you fully and richly.

DEEPER UNDERSTANDINGS

The blessings Moshe pronounced over the Israeli tribes, prior to his death, appear very similar to those uttered by Ya'akov, prior to his death, as recorded in Genesis 49. However, an even greater understanding emerges from Moshe's final exhortation. As we read in verses 3b and 4a, of Deuteronomy 33: *Moses gave us instruction, a possession for the assembly of Ya'akov,* Israel has been to taught to teach, to listen and to hear (obey and follow) the commandments of Adonai. In other words, to follow His Word. As we read in the New Covenant, specifically John 1, the Word to be followed is Adonai YESHUA, our Lord and Messiah.

REUVEN

The two major reasons for the 'blessing' of Reuben have been presented. However, more may be added. In Moshe's prayer, we are led to believe he sees Reuben's or the tribe's decisions not to be sufficient to warrant the tribe's extinction. Thus, the tribe would still exist but in reduced numbers. As far as can be determined, there was never a prophet, king or judge who came from the tribe of Reuben.[87]

Rashi claimed, although the numbers of the tribe of Reuben would diminish, the tribe would never die. Another rationale for the verse comes from Sforno[88], who

---

[87] Guzik, D. *Deuteronomy 33 – Moses blesses the tribes*, Enduring Word, https://enduringword.com/bible-commentary/deuteronomy-33/, accessed 11 December, 2023.

[88] Obediah ben Ya'akov Sforno, Sforno, an Italian rabbi who lived from 1470 to1550. He was a physician, a philosopher and biblical commentator.

151

claimed that the 'blessing' upon Reuben resulted from the tribe's claiming territory on the east side of the Yarden, rather than joining Israel on the west side.

Y'HUDAH

The tribe of Y'hudah was the origin of the Davidic line and the line which led to Messiah YESHUA. The Gemara[89] expressed the blessing of the tribe was the result of Y'hudah having repented of his sins: *Yehuda admitted and was not embarrassed and what was his end? He inherited the world to come.*[90] Notice how the plea rings of ADONAI's support for the continued help in Y'hudah's battles against his foes.

LEVI

As we have read earlier, Exodus 28; Leviticus 28, the Thummim and Urim were objects, possibly stones kept in a pouch,[91] the Levitical priests used in decision making, following the will of ADONAI. Just what stones were used has never been determined. By asking these remain with tribe of Levi, Moshe was proclaiming Levi's eternal and dedicated service to *HaShem*. (The Hebrew word HaShem means the Name and is used often to refer to Adonai.) This position was cemented at the waters of Meribah (Exodus 17) and at Massah (Exodus 17), where the Levites, acting as elders of the nation, supported Moshe. As we see throughout Numbers and Leviticus, the Levites remained true to ADONAI's word, at least until they became corrupted as we read in Judges 17, no matter what the trial placed before them. Thus, they proved worthy of sharing His Word with the nation.

The phrase, *for they kept Your word and maintained Your covenant* Deuteronomy 33:9b, is very important, as it signifies the role that the tribe of Levi had in Israel. They were the teachers of Israel and followed ADONAI's commands to promote His word throughout the nation. Being scattered throughout the other tribes, once they entered the promised land, Levi became the glue which was to hold the nation together.

As we read in Joshua 21, the Levitical priests of their 3 clans received cities and the grasslands surrounding them, throughout the new land, as their accommodations. For example, the families of one portion of the K'hati Levites received 13 cities and their surrounding lands from the tribes of Y'hudah, Shimon and Binyamin. Another portion

---

[89] The Gemara consists of rabbinical commentary of Torah and is found throughout the Talmud, the source of Jewish law.
[90] Sotah 7b:7, Sefaria, https://www.sefaria.org/Sotah.7b.7?lang=bi, accessed 11 December, 2023.
[91] Waltke, B., *Finding the will of God*, Eerdmans Publishing, 2016, Pp. 62-64, Grand Rapids, Michigan.

of the family received 10 cities from the tribes of Efrayim, Dan and the half tribe of M'nasheh. These were the only places the Levites could live and the only property they could own. The Levites were Adonai's holy children, set apart from Israel. Adonai was their inheritance and their role was to serve Him at the Temple.

BINYAMIN

God preserved the tribe of Binyamin and used this tribe to develop His kingdom, as may be seen in Judges, the prophecies of Jeremiah and the writings of the Apostle Paul, who was from the tribe of Binyamin. ADONAI's love for Binyamin may also be seen in His making a Benyamite city the capital of the nation of Israel – Yerushalayim/Jerusalem.

In his blessings of his twelve sons, as we read in Genesis 49:27, Ya'akov called Binyamin a wolf; *he tears his prey. In the morning he devours the prey, and in the evening he divides the plunder.* Although one of the smaller tribes of Israel, Binyamin was a warrior tribe, fierce and warlike.

YOSEF

Reuben and Simeon lost their positions as the first and second sons of Ya'akov, due to their having disgraced themselves. Reuben disgraced himself by sleeping with one of Ya'akov's wives (Genesis 5:22), a clear violation of Torah, and Simeon disgraced himself by joining Levi in the killing of the males of Shechem (Genesis 34:25,26), following the assault upon Dinah, their sister. With these tribes having lost their prominence, Yosef's sons Ephraim and Manasseh were made Ya'akov's sons. The tribe of Ephraim gained eminance by being the largest of all the tribes of Israel.

The phrase, *Such are the ten thousands of Ephraim, and such are the thousands of Manasseh,* refers to Ya'akov's prophetic blessing of Yosef, when he said, as recorded in Genesis 49:22, *Joseph is a fruitful vine, a fruitful vine beside a spring; its branches climb over the wall;* we know Ephraim was the largest tribe of Israel and its size gave it increased status within the nation. History tells us Ephraim led the ten tribes of Israel in the territory of Dan, following the death of King Solomon.

John W. Ritenbaugh[92] has produced an interesting theory about these two nations: *These things just typify the inherent drive of the people of Joseph, a proclivity to expand beyond the frontiers in every endeavor. They are an aggressive and innovative people in science,*

---

[92] Ritenbaugh J.W., Christmas Syncretism and Presumption, Forerunner Magazine, Church of the Great God, December 2001.

industry, education, government, and religion. This is generally beneficial and productive, but in one area, religion, it has profound repercussions. Satan has taken advantage of this characteristic, producing a religion that allows Israelites to think that they are Christian and yet still be free to explore the frontiers of religious thought. I suggest you accept this with a grain of salt, as this follows the line of Replacement Theology, also called supersessionism, held by many Church publishers[93].

ZEBULUN AND ISSACHAR

In Genesis 49:13, Ya'akov blessed Zebulun with these words: *Zebulun will live by the seashore and will be a harbor for ships, and his territory will be next to Sidon.* This tells us that Zebulun was a coastal tribe, who traded with other nations. As mentioned earlier, this also made Zebulun more vulnerable to outside attack than other Israel tribes.

Why did Moshe bless Zebulun before Issachar, even though Issachar was the firstborn son? Interestingly, Ya'akov also blessed Zebulun first, as we read in Exodus 49. We may never know the reason for both Ya'akov and Moahe blessing Zebulun before Issachar; this is one of the mysteries of the Torah. It appears, as mentioned by Charlie Garrett,[94] Zebulun was given access to the Sea of Galilee and the Mediterranean Sea, even though their territory touched neither of these seas. The territory belonging to Issachar did touch the Sea of Galilee and Zebulun had access to it for their trade in fish.

GAD

This blessing begins with a praise for ADONAI, who allowed the tribe to settle on the east side of the Yarden River, as we read in Numbers 32. Positioning them in this way, allowed this aggressive and warlike tribe to better defend the entire nation from attack on their eastern flank.

During the campaign to overtake the promised land from the Cana'anites, Gad occupied somewhat of a leadership role, as Moshe prophesized with *a ruler's portion was assigned there for him.* Another praise for Gad is revealed in the latter part of verse 21: *he carried out the LORD's justice and His ordinances for Israel,* indicating members of the tribe fulfilled their Torah obligations and encouraged others to follow on their path.

---

[93] Missler, C., *Israel and the Church*, Koinonia House, 2016, Coeur d'Alene.
[94] Garrett, C., *Deuteronomy 33:18-22*, The Superior Word, Deuteronomy 33:18-22 (Moses Blesses Israel, Part III) – The Superior Word, accessed 04 July, 2024.

DAN

We first heard a blessing over Dan, the son of Ya'akov from Bilhah, when Ya'akov summarized his life as *He will be a snake by the road, a viper beside the path, that bites the horses' heels so that its rider falls backward.* Genesis 49:17. This indicates the tribe of Dan would be a stumbling block for the nation. It is important to note that Dan is omitted in Revelation 7, where John notes in his vision the gathering of the tribes at the end of ages.

As mentioned earlier, Dan was allotted the territory on the western coast of the land, territory occupied by the Philistines. Apparently, they found these people too difficult to overcome and decided to move to the northern part of the Galilee, slaughtering the original people living there.

Dan lived in the area of Bashan, now known as the Golan Heights. This area has been in the news over the last few years, as it is territory Syria believes belongs to them. There are still fields with land mines, a remnant of the 1973 war, in which Syria invaded the area, inflicting heavy losses on the Israeli army. Israel regained the area and, in the ceasefire agreement of 1974, a UN observation force was stationed there to preserve the peace.

NAPHTALI

Although Naphtali's blessing was short, it is filled with meaning. We see this is verse 23: *Naphtali, enjoying approval, full of the LORD's blessing.* This blessing enshrined in the tribe the riches that lay on the shores of the Galilee. The upper Galilee is a rich and fertile area, with much of Israel's exporting produce derived from there. In Isaiah 9:1,2, we may see Isaiah's prophecy of ADONAI YESHUA walking through the territory of Naphtali, in the words: *But in the future He will bring honor to the Way of the Sea, to the land east of the Jordan, and to Galilee of the nations. The people walking in darkness have seen a great light; a light has dawned on those living in the land of darkness.*

ASHER

By using the phrase, *May Asher be the most blessed of the sons; may he be the most favored among his brothers and dip his foot in olive oil,* Moshe is prophesizing that the tribe of Asher will be more favourable blessed than other tribes and be given more material wealth. Given the tribe was located on the coast, near where Tel Aviv now stands, it became a sea faring tribe, trading with other nations. ADONAI granted Asher protection from attack and invasion from elsewhere.

As Herman Hoeh[95] informs us, Simeon did have a small piece of land south of Y'hudah. At the time Israel separated from the tribes of Y'hudah and Binyamin, the a great portion of the tribe of Simeon went with them. Those who were left, joined Y'hudah. It is suggested that when Israel was taken into present day Europe, the members of Simeon were called Senones.

As we have learned, Ya'akov blessed his 12 sons, while on his death-bed in Egypt. It will be profitable to compare the two sets of blessings:

YA'AKOV'S BLESSINGS GENESIS 49 MOSHE'S BLESSINGS DEUTERONOMY 33

Reuben Verses 3 and 4	*you are my firstborn, my strength and the firstfruits of my virility . . . you will no longer excel, because you got into your father's bed and you defiled it.*	Reuben Verse 6	*Let Reuben live and not die though his people become few.*
Simeon And Levi Verses 5 to 7	*Simeon and Levi are brothers; their knives are vicious weapons. May I never enter their council; may I never join their assembly.*	Levi Verses 8 to 11	*Your Thummim and Urim belong to Your faithful one; You tested him at Massah and contended with him at the waters of Meribah.*
Judah Verses 8 to 12	*Judah, your brothers will praise you. Your hand will be on the necks of your enemies; your father's sons will bow down to you.*	Judah Verse 7	*LORD, hear Judah's cry and bring him to his people. He fights for his cause with his own hands, but may You be a help against his foes.*
Zebulun Verse 13	*Zebulun will live by the seashore and will be a harbor for ships, and his territory will be next to Sidon.*	Zebulun Verses 18 ands 19	*Rejoice, Zebulun, in your journeys, and Issachar, in your tents.*
Issachar Verses 14 and 15	*Issachar is a strong donkey lying down between the saddlebags. He saw that his resting place was good and that the land was pleasant, so he leaned his shoulder to bear a load and became a forced laborer.*	Issachar Verses 18 and 19	*They summon the peoples to a mountain; there they offer acceptable sacrifices. For they draw from the wealth of the seas and the hidden treasures of the sand.*

---

[95] Hoeh, H., *Location of the Tribes of Israel*, Herbert W. Armstrong, Location of the Tribes of Israel (hwalibrary. com) accessed 05 July, 2024.

Dan Verses 16 to 18	Dan will judge his people as one of the tribes of Israel. He will be a snake by the road, a viper beside the path, that bites the horses' heels so that its rider falls backward. I wait for Your salvation, LORD.	Dan Verse 22	Dan is a young lion, leaping out of Bashan.
Gad Verse 19	Gad will be attacked by raiders, but he will attack their heels.	Gad Verses 20 and 21	The one who enlarges Gad's territory will be blessed. He lies down like a lion and tears off an arm or even a head.
Asher Verse 20	Asher's food will be rich, and he will produce royal delicacies.	Asher Verses 24 and 25	May Asher be the most blessed of the sons; may he be the most favored among his brothers and dip his foot in olive oil. May the bolts of your gate be iron and bronze, and your strength last as long as you live.
Naphtali Verse 21	Naphtali is a doe set free that bears beautiful fawns.	Naphtali Verse 23	Naphtali, enjoying approval, full of the LORD's blessing, take possession to the west and the south.
Joseph Verses 22 to 26	Joseph is a fruitful vine, a fruitful vine beside a spring; its branches climb over the wall.	Joseph Verses 13 to 17	May his land be blessed by the LORD with the dew of heaven's bounty and the watery depths that lie beneath . . . Such are the ten thousands of Ephraim, and such are the thousands of Manasseh.
Benjamin Verse 27	Benjamin is a wolf; he tears his prey. In the morning he devours the prey, and in the evening he divides the plunder.	Benjamin Verse 12	The LORD's beloved rests securely on Him. He shields him all day long, and he rests on His shoulders.

FACE-TO-FACE

The phrase, face-to-face, is mentioned many times throughout both the Hebrew and the Apostolic Scriptures. In Deuteronomy 34:10, printed above, we see this phrase referring to Adonai's relationship with Moshe. Face-to-Face does not mean literally standing face-to-face. This phrase has a very deep meaning in Hebrew. The phrase, *panim el-panim*, brings with it an understanding of intimate understandings of one's character, when in relationship. This is the same understanding married couples have in close relationship with each other. Thus, when Moshe writes that he and Adonai met face-to-face, it means they both had an intimate understanding of each others' character. How awesome is that for us to contemplate in our growth towards our LORD and MASTER.

This completes the Weekly Readings of HaSefer D'Varim.

Hazak, hazak, v'nit'chazek!

Be strong, be strong, and let us be strengthened!

Conclusion

In our journey through HaSefer D'Varim our leader Moshe introduces us to the life instructions of our Father and King, YHVH, Avinu Malkainu. These instructions cover the ethical, moral, legal and many of the ceremonial instructions presented in the first four books of Torah. As we can see, these come to us through both stories and narrative.

Throughout the book we are led into several key themes, including our need to trust ADONAI, to obey His commands and to reach for Him when we are in need of assistance. When we fail to address these needs within our daily lives, we fall into the trap of idolatry. This is of our own making, of course, often, I believe, with the influence of satan; however, once in these traps it is virtually impossible for us to get ourselves out; only with Adonai's help will we succeed in climbing out of our pits (John 10:28; Psalm 40:2).

What we sometimes fail to see is that while these needs seem philosophical and abstract in our modern age, we are required to put them into practice on an every day basis. When we are in situations that are difficult for us, we need to trust ADONAI to aid us, direct us and, sometimes, pull us out of impossible circumstances. Then we thank Him for being there for us, when everything turns out the way He had planned. How many of us forget to thank Him, when our problem is resolved in ways we could never imagine. With each task we need to go before Him and ask Him for support, guidance and protection, relying on Him to help us choose wisely, according to His will.

All of us have limits to our abilities and we need to recognize and accept these before we turn to Him for guidance and leadership. Moshe understood this and was in constant communion with ADONAI always and especially when faced with rebellions from Israel and there were many.

Throughout our life journeys we meet many different people. Some of these challenge us. It is easy for us to show respect for those we deem 'correct'. How often do we show respect for those who are often impolite and disrespectful to us? This is one of His teachings. You may remember what He said in Matthew 7:12 - *Therefore, whatever you want others to do for you, do also the same for them -- this is the Law and the Prophets.*

All of us, in many different capacities, exercise authority. Whether this is in a family or in a small business, a classroom or a large company, the principles are similar. We show respect for all and treat everyone under our authority as worthy.

Similarly, we are under the authority of others. Our Master, ADONAI YESHUA, is our key authority. We answer to Him now and forever. No matter who our authority is, we must be diligent in following their commands or orders (Romans 13:1). Moshe tells us we are ultimately doing things for ADONAI. No matter who gives us our orders, we must assume we are working for our Ruler.

We have been told in both Deuteronomy and in the teachings of ADONAI YESHUA, we are stewards of all ADONAI gives us. It is up to us to ensure that we are wise in how we use the resources He gives us and generous, when we share resources with others less fortunate that ourselves.

Moshe also teaches us to be mindful of others in our business dealings. It is incumbent upon us to be faithfully honest in our transactions. He watches us constantly and, if we show dishonesty towards others, we will eventually be punished. Only His grace, mercy and goodness may relieve us of the consequences of our misbehaviour.

Each of us has been given a commission in our daily lives, as we read in both the Hebrew and Apostolic Scriptures. In all our interactions we are to work towards the transformation of ourselves, our families, our communities (home and work) and our nations to eradicate idolatrous behaviours, such as slavery and the exploitation of others, corruption, injustice and the indifference we witness of others to the lack of resources of workers and the poor. are we indeed announcing the Good News as Yeshua has asked us to do?

But, throughout all of Deuteronomy, we are being taught we have a responsibility to seek ADONAI and rest in our relationship with Him. Remember Moshe's words to us, recorded in Deuteronomy 4:29, *you will search for the LORD your God, and you will find Him when you seek Him with all your heart and all your soul.* In every task we endeavour, there is a risk of failure. When we do stumble, and we all do, we must not focus on the need to do better next time but the desire to do better, as we are His feet, hands, ears and eyes, and to accept this 'failure' as an invitation to grow, learn and draw closer to Him.

Finally, it is important for us to understand that ADONAI'S commands for Israel then and us now are not impossible lists of demands upon us but His desire for us to come as close to Him as we are able and as our desires dictate and rely upon Him to ensure we more closely meet His standards, as we read in Romans 12:2 - *Do not be conformed to this age, but be transformed by the renewing of your mind, so that you may discern what is the good, pleasing, and perfect will of God.* Remember what Moshe told us in Deuteronomy 10:12, *And now, Israel, what does the Lᴏʀᴅ your God ask of you except to fear the Lᴏʀᴅ your God by walking in all His ways, to love Him, and to worship the Lᴏʀᴅ your God with all your heart and all your soul.* And may we all respond to this with Amen, Amen.

May the God of Avraham, Yitzchak and Ya'akov bless
you fully and richly as you walk on His path.

GLOSSARY

Word	Hebrew	English Translation	Description
		A	
Abba	אַבָּא	Father	An intimate word used by children for their fathers.
Acharei Mot	אַחֲרֵי מוֹת	After the death.	Title of the 6th weekly reading of the Book of Leviticus.
Achat	אַחַת	One.	The one of.
Adah	עָדָה	Nobility, adornment	Wife of Lamech and daughter of Jamal.
Adar	אֲדָר	The 12th month of the biblical calendar.	The month when Purim is celebrated.
Adom	אדמה	Man	The man created by Adonai in Genesis 2. For some reason, the translators of the Bible claimed his name was Adam.
Adonai	אֲדֹנָי	My Lord	Adonai has come to mean 'the Lord'
Adonai Tzivaot	יְהֹוָה צְבָאוֹת	Lord of Hosts.	First mentioned in Joshua 5.
Adullam	עֲדֻלָּם	Hiding place	a major Cana'anite region to which Y'hudah moved, after Yosef was sold to the Yisma'elim.
Agag	אֲגַג	King of the nation of Amalek	Spared by King Sha'ul, when he attacked the Amaleki on the orders of the prophet Samuel.

Word	Hebrew	English Translation	Description
Ahavah	אַהֲבָה	Love.	Connotes loving kindness, steadfast bonding, covenant commitment, intimate friendship
Ahmose		Child of the moon	Pharaoh and founder of the eighteen dynasty of Egypt.
Akeidah Yitzchak	יִצְחָק עֲקֵדָה	Binding of Yitzchak	Mentioned in Genesis 22, Avraham told by Adonai to take Yitzchak to Mount Moriah and sacrifice him.
Aliyah	עליה	Ascent or going up.	The word used to describe a person relocating to Israel or going up to the bimah to read Torah.
Amalek	עֲמָלֵק	Descendent of Esav; his prosperity	The name of the nation of Amalek, the fiercest of Israel's enemies. Eliminated when Haman and his sons were hanged for attempting to kill the Jews in Persia.
Amos	עָמוֹס	Burden, carrying a weight.	Amos was a minor prophet of Israel in the 8th. Century BCE.
Ammon	עַמּוֹן	Teacher or builder.	The nation of people Moshe & Israel met on their route to the promised land on the east side of the Jordan River.
Amorite	אֱמֹרִי	Talkers.	Inhabitants of Cana'an and a foe of Israel all through its existence.
Anakim	עֲנָקִים		Peoples living in the southern area of Cana'an, in the territory ruled by Edom and Moab.
'ar	עָר	Awakening; a place guarded by a watch.	The capital city of the Moabite empire.
aramaic	אֲרָמִית	aramaic belongs to the Northwest group of the Semitic	language family, which also includes the mutually intelligible Canaanite languages such as Hebrew, Edomite, Moabite, Ekronite, Sutean, and Phoenician, as well as Amorite and Ugaritic.

Word	Hebrew	English Translation	Description
aramean	אֲרַמִים	Descendants of aram, son of Shem, son of Noah.	People who lived in the Levant and spoke aramaic. Not a centralized people group.
Aravah	עֲרָבָה	Leafy branch of the willow tree.	One of the 4 species used during Sukkot.
arnon	אַרְנֹן	Swift; roaring; rushing stream;	a river east of the Jordan River, known now as Wadi Mujib.
Aseret Hadevarim	הַדְּבָרִים עֲשֶׂרֶת	Ten Words.	Known also as the Ten Commandments, given to Israel at Mt. Simai.
Aseneth	אָסְנַת	She belongs to; is the servant of.	The Egyptian woman who Pharoah gave to Yosef as his wife
Asher	אָשֵׁר	Happy, blessing	Ya'akov's eighth son from Zilpah.
Asherim poles	אֲשֵׁרִים	Asherim poles	are trees or poles placed near Cana'anite places of worship. Honour the goddess Ashera.
Av	אָב	Father.	The 5th month of the biblical calendar, usually late July or August.
Avim	עַוִּים	People living in the south west corner of the Mediterranean Sea;	portion of Philistia.
Avimelekh	אֲבִימֶלֶךְ	My father reigns	Generic name for all Philistine kings.
Avinu	אָבִינוּ	Our Father.	Title of Adonai used in many Jewish and Messianic prayers.
Aviv	אָבִיב	Spring.	The first year of the biblical calendar usually comes in late March or early April.
Avodah Zarah	עבודה זרה	Foreign	worship, idolatry.
Avram	אַבְרָם	Exalted father	The original name of Abraham before Adonai changed it to Avraham.

WORD	HEBREW	ENGLISH TRANSLATION	DESCRIPTION
Avraham	אַבְרָהָם	father of many	Adonai changed Avram's name, after he was circumcised.

B

WORD	HEBREW	ENGLISH TRANSLATION	DESCRIPTION
Ba'al	בַּעַל	Owner or lord;	title given to one of the deity of Cana'an.
Balak	בָּלָק	Devastator, empty, wasting.	The king of Moab described in Numbers. The title of the 7th Parashah/weekly re4ading of the Book of Numbers.
Baruch	בָּרוּךְ	Blessed	The first word of almost every Hebrew prayer.
Bashan	בָּשָׁן	*Smooth or light soil.*	*The kingdom of Og, east of the Jordan River.*
Batyah		Daughter of God	The daughter of the pharaoh at the time of Moshe.
Bavel	בבל	Confusion	The word used to describe the tower built by the people who descended from Adom and Chava.
B'ha'aloha/ Behaalotecha	בְּהַעֲלֹתְךָ	When you step up.	The title of the 3rd Parashah/ weekly re4ading of the Book of Numbers.
Behar/B'har	בְּהַר	On the mount	The title of the 9th weekly reading of the Book of Leviticus.
Bechukottai/ B'chukotti	בְּחֻקֹּתַי	By My regulations.	The 10th and final weekly reading of the Book of Leviticus.
BeMidbar/ B'Midbar	בְּמִדְבַּר	In the wilderness.	The title of the Book of Numbers and the first Parashah/the weekly reading.
Bethuel/Beit-El	בְּתוּאֵל	House of God	The name of Lavan's father.
Bikkurim	בִּכּוּרִים	First Fruits.	The second day of Hag Ha Matzah, the Festival of Unleavened Bread, usually in late March or April, when the barley harvest started. Also recognized as the resurrection day of Adonai Yeshua.

WORD	HEBREW	ENGLISH TRANSLATION	DESCRIPTION
Bilhah	בִּלְהָה	unworried	Rifka's servant given to Ya'akov.
Binyamin/ Binyamin	בִּנְיָמִין	Son of the south, right hand	The 12th son of Ya'akov from Rachel. Rachel died giving birth to Binyamin.
Bo	בּוֹא		He lived, Enter Yosef and his brothers are reconciled after the death of their father, Ya'akov. The title of the 3rd. Weekly Reading in Exodus.
B'resheit	בְּרֵאשִׁית	In the beginning	The Hebrew title of the Book of Genesis
Brachah	בְּרָכָה	Blessing.	Portion of the title of the final weekly reading of Deuteronomy.
Brit Chadashah	ברית חדשה	New Covenant	The name of the writings of the Apostles, Luke, and Jude.
B'shalach	בְּשַׁלַּח	When he let go.	The title of the 3rd Parashah of the Book of Exodus

C

WORD	HEBREW	ENGLISH TRANSLATION	DESCRIPTION
Cana'an	כְּנַעַן		The land Israel was given in Covenant by Adonai.
Chava	חַוָּה	Breath of life	The name (Eve) given to the woman created to be man's helpmate, in Genesis 2.
Chag	חַג	Holiday/Festival	Every biblical holiday is preceded by chag. Chag HaMatzah; Chag Sukkot; etc.
Chukkiim	חוקים	Statutes or decrees.	These have no discernable rationale. They are followed because Adonai commanded them.
Chen	חֵן	grace, favour and beauty	Often used in the First Covenant to describe Adonai's grace to whomever He wishes.

Word	Hebrew	English Translation	Description
D			
Dan	דָּן	to judge	Ya'akov's fifth son and Rifka's first child. The ancestor of the tribe of Dan.
David	דָּוִד	Beloved	The king of Israel after Sha'ul, approximately 1,000 to 962 BCE.
Devarim/ D'Varim	דְּבָרִים	things/words	The title of the 5th book of Torah and the 1st parashah of Deuteronomy.
Dinah	דִּינָה	Judged, vindicated	Ya'akov's seventh child from Leah.
E			
Ebal	עֵיבָל		Mountain north of Mt. Gerizim, near Nablus and Shechem on West Bank of the Jordan River.
Echad	אֶחָד	One.	Unity, being many parts but one.
Eden	עֵדֶן	Delightful place	The first garden created by Adonai to house animals of the world. The location is thought to be in what is now the head of the Persian Gulf and extending into Jordan.
Edom	אֱדֹם	Red	The nickname for Esav, Ya'akov's brother; the name of a group of people from Esav.
Edot	עֵדְוֹת	Testimonials	Rules of Jewish festivals, commemorating important events in Jewish history.
Efrat	אֶפְרָת	Fruitful, Honoured	The place where Ya'akov buried Rachel. Close to Bethlechem
Ekev	עֵקֶב	If you follow, because	The title of the 3rd parashah of Deuteronomy.

Word	Hebrew	English Translation	Description
Elah	אֵלָה	The Terebinth tree.	Y'hudah moved to the region overlooking the Elah Valley, where David faced Goliath.
Eliezer	אֱלִיעֶזֶר	My God is help	The name of Avraham's servant, who went to Haran to find a wife for Yitzchak.
Elohim	אֱלֹהִים	God or Godhood	The word used for YHVH, when His name is not pronounced.
Emor	אֱמֹר	Speak	The title of the 8th weekly re4ading of the Book of Leviticus.
Emori	אֱמֹרִי	Mountain dwellers	The Amorite nation defeated by Moshe, as reported in Numbers 21.
Emunah	אמונה	Trust-in-action,	meaning faith translated into faithfulness.
Enoch	חֲנוֹךְ	Train or initiate	Son of Jarad and father of Methuselah
Ephron	עֶפְרוֹן		*Singing bird, fawn-like the son of Zochar, a Hittite, from whom Avraham bought the firld and cave at Machpelah.*
Ephraim	אֶפְרָיִם	Fruitful	The second son of Yosef.
Er	עֵר	Awake	The first son of Y'hudah and Shua.
Esav	עֵשָׂו	hairy	Esav was the first son born to Ya'akov from Rifka.
Ever	עבר	Cross over or pass through.	The ancestor of Avraham and the Hebrews.

G

Word	Hebrew	English Translation	Description
Gad	גָּד	Fortune, Luck	Ya'akov's son from Zilpah.
Gadol	גָּדוֹל	Great	Adjective describing anything perceived as being superior.

WORD	HEBREW	ENGLISH TRANSLATION	DESCRIPTION
Gemara	גמרא	To finish/complete.	The name given to the Oral Torah passed down from Moshe orally. It was not allowed to be written down until Judah the Prince compiles the Mishna in 200 CE (approx.)
Get	גט	Divorce document.	The get originated in Moshe's time designed to satisfy the hard-hearted Israelite men.
Gan	גַּן	Garden	Gan Eden, the Garden of Eden.
Gerizim	גְּרִזִים		Mountain in Samaria near Nablus and Shechem, on the West Bank of the Jordan River.
Gershom	גֵּרְשֹׁם	A sojourner there	The first son of Moshe & Zipporah.
Gibeon	גִּבְעוֹן		Name of a nation of people living in Cana'an, when Israel entered the land.
Golan	גּוֹלָן	Passage, Revolution	An early biblical town known for the works of Josephus (1st C. CE) and Eusebius (4TH C. CE).
Gomorrah	עֲמֹרָה	a place known for vice and depravity	The second city destroyed by Adonai in Genesis 13.
Goshen	גֹּשֶׁן	Fertile land	The territory in the Nile Delta occupied by Israel, when he and his people arrived in Egypt.
Goyim	גּוֹי	Nations, plural of goy.	All nations are goyim; however, when Jewish people use goyim, they are referring to non-Jewish people.

H

WORD	HEBREW	ENGLISH TRANSLATION	DESCRIPTION
Ha'atzinu	הַאֲזִינוּ	Listen, plural.	The title of the 9th Parashah of Deuteronomy.
Hagadol	הַגָּדוֹל	The Great.	Adjective used to describe the head priest or a day of honour.

Word	Hebrew	English Translation	Description
Hagar	הָגָר	flight, forsaken	Hagar was the mother of Ismael, before Sarah bore Yitzchak.
Hakadosh Baruch Hu	הַקָּדוֹשׁ בָּרוּךְ הוּא	The Holy One;	blessed be He. Used as a prefix for many Jewish prayers.
Hamor	חֲמוֹר	an ass	The father of the man who raped Dinah, Ya'akov's daughter, and claimed her as his wife.
Haran	הָרָן	Mountaineer	Haran was Avraham's brother – father Terah.
Hasefer	הַסֵּפֶר	The book	The Hebrew word for 'the book'.
Hashem/ HaShem	הַשֵּׁם	The Name	Jewish people use 'the Name' for God, rather than pronouncing His holy Name.
Hayyei Sarah	חַיֵּי שָׂרָה	The life of Sarah	The parashah of B'resheit (23:1 to 25:18) dealing with Abraham's wife.
Het	חֵת	sin, faults	The name of the owner of the Machpelah caves; the 8th letter of the Hebrew alphabet.
Heshbon	חֶשְׁבּוֹן	The royal city of Sichon, king of the Amorites;	Adonai caused great distress in the minds of the Amorites, as Israel approached the city.
Hittite	חִתִּי	Descendent of Heth.	One of the nations inhabiting Cana'an.
Hivite	חוים	Tent Villagers.	Inhabitants of Cana'an when Israel entered the Holy Land.
Horim	הורים	Parents;	the name of the people living at Mt. Se'ir who were replaced by the Edomites.
Hosea	הוֹשֵׁעַ	Salvation.	Also known as Osee, son of Beery. Hosea was a minor prophet in Israel in the 8th Century BCE.

Word	Hebrew	English Translation	Description
Hovat Yair	יָאִיר חַנֵּת	Reveal enlighten.	A farming settlement in the West Bank of Israel.
Hukkat	חֻקַּת	Regulation	The title of the 6th Parahsah/weekly reading of the Book of Numbers.
Hyksos		Shepherd kings	The first name of the Hebrews in Cana'an.

I

Word	Hebrew	English Translation	Description
Ishmael	יִשְׁמָעֵאל	God will hear	Ishmael was the first born son of Avraham from Hagar, Sarah's Egyptian servant girl.
Isaiah	יְשַׁעְיָהוּ	YHVH is Salvation.	Prophet of Israel in 8th Century.
Issachar	יִשָּׂשכָר	There is recompense.	Ya'akov's ninth son from Leah.

J

Word	Hebrew	English Translation	Description
Jebusite	יְבוּסִי	Trodden underfoot.	Inhabitants of Cana'an when Israel entered the Holy Land.
Joel	יוֹאֵל	YHVH is God; determined.	There is no consensus regarding his birth; assumed to be in the 9th Century BCE. Was thought to be one of the minor prophets of Israel.
Jonah	יוֹנָה	Dove/pigeon.	Prophet of Israel in the Northern Kingdom of Israel in 8th Century.

K

Word	Hebrew	English Translation	Description
Kadesh	קָדֵשׁ		An ancient settlement located in southern Y'hudah, at the southern border of Cana'an.
Kadesh-Barnea	קדש ברנע	Sacred desert of wandering	Part of the territory allotted to Y'hudah, situated in the far south of Cana'an.

WORD	HEBREW	ENGLISH TRANSLATION	DESCRIPTION
Kalev/Caleb	כָּלֵב	Dog	One of the 12 spies who crossed into the promised land, as reported in Numbers 13, and who gave a positive report about the land.
Kayin	קַיִן	Acquire or Possess	The name given to Chava's first son.
Kedoshim/ K'doshim	קְדֹשִׁים	Holy ones.	Title of the 7th weekly reading of the Book of Leviticus.
Kena'an	כְּנַעַן	Cana'an humbled, subdued	The region where Ya'akov and his family settled before moving to Goshen, Egypt.
Ketuvim	כְּתוּבִים	The Writings.	Chronicles, Psalms, Proverbs, Job, Ezra and Nehemiah form the Ketuvim.
Kiddushin	קִידוּשִׁין	An engagement.	A tractate of Mishna and Talmud focusing on legal provisions attached to engagement and marriage.
Ki Tetze	כִּי־תֵצֵא	When you go	The title of the 6th parashah of Deuteronomy.
K'turah/Keturah	קְטוּרָה	Incense, perfumed	The second wife of Avraham, after Sarah's death.
Ki Tavo	כִּי־תָבוֹא	When you enter	The title of the 7th parashah of Deuteronomy.
Ki Tissa	כִּי תִשָּׂא	When you elevate	The title of the 9th Parashah of the Book of Exodus.
Kohanim	כֹּהֲנִים	Priests	The plural of Kohen. The name given to all the priests on duty at the Temple.
Kohen/Cohen	כֹּהֵן		Priest, with reference to Aaronic priesthood.

Word	Hebrew	English Translation	Description
Korach	קֹרַח	Baldness, ice, hail	The title of the 4th Parashah/weekly reading of the Book of Numbers. The name of the family of Levites who rebelled against Moshe & Aharon at Mt. Sinai.
Korban	קָרְבָּן	Drawing near.	The name given to any sacrifice presented to Adonai on the Alter.
Kyriat-arba	קִרְיַת־אַרְבַּע	Town of the Four	Originally an oasis south of Hebron.

L

Word	Hebrew	English Translation	Description
Laban/Lavan	לָבָן	White Rifka's brother.	The man who hired Ya'akov for his daughter, Rachel
Leah	לֵאָה	delicate, weary	Ya'akov's first wife, Lavan's sister.
Lemekh	לֶמֶךְ	Striker down or strong youth	The last of the descendants of Cain.
Lech L'kha	לֶךְ לֹךָ	Get yourself out	Adonai's words to Abram while he was still in Mesopotamia.
Levi	לֵוִי	joined to.	Ya'akov's son from Leah. Levi was the ancestor of the tribe of Levi, found in Exodus to Deuteronomy. Founded the tribe of Levites.
Likkutei Sichos	לקוטי שיחות	Collected Talks.	Contains the scope and core of Rabbi Mendel Schneerson, the Lubavitcher Rebbe.
Lot	לוֹט	Avram's nephew.	Lot was the ancestor of the Amorites.
Lyar	אִייָר	Ani Hashem Rophecha -- I am Hashem your Healer.	The 2nd month of the year, beginning with 01 Aviv.

WORD	HEBREW	ENGLISH TRANSLATION	DESCRIPTION
		M	
Machanayim	מַחֲנָיִם	Two camps	A settlement located east of the River Jordan, where Ya'akov encountered angels.
Machpelah	מַכְפֵּלָה	Double Cave	Where Avraham, Sarah, Yitzchak and Ya'akov are buried. Located near Hebron.
Malachi	מַלְאָכִי	Messenger of God	The last book of the prophets in the Tanakh.
Malachim	מלאכים	Angels/messengers	Agents of Adonai who brings His Word to humans.
Malkeinu	מַלְכֵּנוּ	Our King.	The term our King is used in many Jewish and Messianic prayers.
Mamre	מַמְרֵא	Lusty Oak	Where Avraham struck his tent and was visited by the three heavenly messengers; where Israel rested in their flight from Egypt.
Mamzer	מַמְזֵר	Child of incest, bastard	Any child born out of wedlock.
Manasseh/ Menashe	מְנַשֶּׁה	*To forget*	*The first son of Yosef.*
Manna	מָן		Edible substance Adonai provided Israel in their 40 years of wandering. Found in Exodus 16 and Numbers 11.
Masa'ei	מַסְעֵי	Stages/Journeys	The title of the 10th Parashah/weekly reading of the Book of Numbers.
Matot	מַטּוֹת	Tribes.	The title of the 9th Parashah/weekly reading of the Book of Numbers.
Matzah	מַצָּה	Flat bread made without yeast or other leaven.	The bread served during the Festival of Matzah, Hag HaMatzo - Leviticus 23.

Word	Hebrew	English Translation	Description
Metzora/M'tzora	מְצֹרָע	Person afflicted with tzara'at.	The 5th weekly reading of the Book of Leviticus.
Midian	מִדְיָן	Strife	The 4th son of Avraham and Keturah; the land that Moshe escaped to when he fled Egypt at the age of 40.
Midrash	מִדְרָשׁ	Textual interpretation or study.	Expansive exergies of Torah. It is a collection of over 20 volumes.
Mikketz	מִקֵץ	At the end	Yosef elevated to prominence in pharaoh's court
Micah	מִיכָיְהוּ	Who is like God?	Prophet of Israel in 6th Century Israel. One of the minor prophets.
Midbar	מִדְבָּר	Driving (animals), pasture.	Sefer Midbar is the Book of Numbers.
Mikketz	מִקֵץ	At the end	Title of the 10th Parashah.
Mishna	מִשְׁנָה	A collection of Jewish traditions;	often called the Oral Law.
Mishpatim	מִשְׁפָּטִים	Laws, judgments	The 6th Parashah of the Book of Exodus
Mo'av/Moab	מוֹאָב		Who is your father? Water of a father. The plains of Mo'av was the home of the Moabites, in the southern potion of modern Jordan. Moshe stood on Mt. Mo'av, on the day he died.
Moriah	מֹרִיָה	A combination of ya'ah, to see, and Yah, God.	The mount upon which Jerusalem now sits.
Moshe	מֹשֶׁה	Saviour, liberator, deliverer; also drawn from the water	The leader of the Israelites as they exited Egypt and wandered in the wilderness.
Moshichainu/ Mashichainu			Our Messiah/Our Anointed One Means the same as the English Christ

Word	Hebrew	English Translation	Description
Munius		Drawn from/ pulled out	The name given to Moshe by his Egyptian mother, Batyah
Myriam/Miriam			Wished-for child; sea of bitterness; bitter

N

Word	Hebrew	English Translation	Description
Nachum	נַחוּם	Comforter	One of the minor prophets of Israel in and around Capernaum in northern Galilee.
Naso נ	שֹׁא	To Take	The title of the 2nd weekly reading/ Parashah of the Book of Numbers.
Nefesh	נֶפֶשׁ	Soul	Refers to that portion of humans in constant communications with Adonai.
Nevi'im	נְבִיאִים	The Prophets.	The former prophets include Joshua, Judges, Samuel and Kings and the latter prophets include Isaiah, Jeremiah, Ezekiel and the 12 Minor Prophets.
Noach/Noah	נֹחַ	Peace, comfort	The name of the builder of the ark.
Naphtali/Naftali	נַפְתָּלִי	My struggle	Ya'akov's sixth son from Bilhah.
Nitzavim	נִצָּבִים	Ones standing	The 8th parashah of the Book of Deuteronomy.
Nun	נוּן	Fish	Father of Y'hoshua, who received the leadership of Israel after the death of Moshe.
Og	עוֹג	Bread baked in ashes	The king of the Amorite nation of Bashan, killed by Moshe during the battle of Edrei – Numbers 21.
Omer	עֹמֶר	Unit of dry measure equal to 30.3 litres approx.	Also translated as a sheaf/bundle of grain. Counting the Omer means counting the days between the Festival of Matzo and Shavu'ot, the time of the wheat harvest.

Word	Hebrew	English Translation	Description
Onan	אוֹנָן	Strong	The second son of Y'hudah and Shua.

P

Word	Hebrew	English Translation	Description
Paddan-aram	פַּדַּן אֲרָם	field of aram	The place where Isaac's brother-in-law, Lavan, lived.
Parashah	פָּרָשָׁה	Portion, Plural - Parashot	The weekly reading of the Torah read by all Jewish people on Shabbat.
P'nei El	עַל פְּנֵי	Face of God	The place where Ya'akov wrestled with the Man of God.
P'kudei	פְּקוּדֵ	Amounts of	Title of the 11th Parashah of the Book of Exodus.
Pinchas	פִּינְחָס	Phinehas.	The title of the 8th Parashah/weekly reading of the Book of Numbers.
Perizzite	פְּרִזִּי	Wilding, Rural.	Inhabitants of Cana'an when Israel entered the promised land.
Pesach	פֶּסַח	Passover.	Held on the 14th of Aviv/Nissan. Sometime in late March or April.
Pikuach nefesh	פִּיקוּחַ נפש	Sanctity of life.	Principle of Torah in which Adonai claims sanctifying life is paramount, even greater than Torah.
Pisgah	פִּסְגָּה	Summit.	Known as Mt. Nebo. Located in Jordan, part of the Abarim mountain range.
Potifar	פּוֹטִיפַר	Egyptian name does not translate into Hebrew	The captain of Pharaoh's guard who purchased Yosef as his slave.

Q

Word	Hebrew	English Translation	Description
		R	
ra'ah	רָעָה	to know	This word means to have an intimate knowledge of a person's character.
Rachel	רָחֵל	ewe	The second wife of Ya'akov.
Re-eh	רְאֵה	see	The title of the 4th parashah of Deuteronomy.
Refa'im	רְפָאִים	*Ancient race of giants;*	*the people the 12 spies discovered in Cana'an, when they went into the land – Numbers 13.*
Rephidim/Refidim	רְפִידִם	Place of rest.	Israel defeated the Amalekites at Refidim. This was also the place where Moshe struck the rock, at Adonai's command, to bring forth water.
Reuben/Reuven	רְאוּבֵן	See, a son.	First of Ya'akov's sons from Leah.
Rifka	רִבְקָה	Rebecca	Rifka was the wife of Yitzchak and the mother of Esav and Ya'akov.
		S	
Sadducee	צְדוּקִים	Religious group of Judeans living at the time of Yeshua, in the period 2nd Century BCE to 70 CE.	The sadducees were eliminated when the Romans destroyed the temple in 70 CE.
Sarai	שָׂרַי	woman of strength, princess	The name of Avraham's wife before the birth of Ishmael.
Seder	סֵדֶר	*Dinner.*	*The meal held at the time of Pesach/ Passover. This is a combined meal and service.*
Sefer	סִפְרֵי	Book	All the books of the Bible in the Hebrew and the Apostolic Scriptures may be called Sefer or Seferim (plural).

Word	Hebrew	English Translation	Description
Se'ir	שֵׂעִיר	Rough, hairy	The land south of Israel, where Yitzhak and his family lived.
Seth	שֵׁת	Appointed or Placed.	The third son of Adom and Chava.
Shabbat	שבת		Seventh day of Rest first mentioned by Adonai in Genesis 1.
Sha'ul	שָׁאוּל	Asked for, prayed for.	Saul, the first king of Israel; the Hebrew name of the Apostle Paul.
Shavu'ot	שָׁבוּעוֹת	Festival of Weeks.	Held 7 weeks after Hag HaMatzo, the Festival of Unleavened Bread – usually in June. Commemorates Israel receiving the 10 Commandments at Mt. Sinai.
Sheetim	שִׁטִים	A community in Southern Israel, located in the arabah valley.	The original area was where women of Moav infiltrated Israel and seduced men to worship ba'al of Peor – Number 25:1-4.
Shekhem	שְׁכֶם	Shoulder,	The seat of a person's interests. The city named for the son of Hamor, who raped Dinah, Ya'akov's daughter and claimed her for his wife.
Shelah	שֵׁלָה	Petition	The third son of Y'hudah and Shua
Shema	שְׁמַע	Hear and obey.	The title of the holy prayer of Israel, recited three times a day. The prayer is found in Deuteronomy 6.
Shemini	שְׁמִינִי	Eighth	3rd weekly reading of the Book of Leviticus
Shemitah/ Sh'mittah	שְׁמִטָּה	The seventh year of a field.	On this 7th year, the field was to rest and return to its initial fertility, according to Adonai's Word. Exodus 23; Leviticus 25; Deuteronomy 15.
Shemot	שְׁמוֹת	Names	The second book of Torah. The story of the Exodus.

WORD	HEBREW	ENGLISH TRANSLATION	DESCRIPTION
Shiloh	שִׁילֹו	Town in Portion of Ephraim.	Also a Messianic title. Shiloh was the place where the Tabernacle was placed until the Temple was built by King Solomon.
Shimon/Simeon	שִׁימוֹן	Hearing	Ya'akov's second son from Leah.
Shlach L'kha	שְׁלַח-לְךָ	Sent on your behalf	The title of the 4th Parashah/weekly reading of the Book of Numbers.
Shoftim	שֹׁפְטִים	Judges	The title 4th parashah of the book of Deuteronomy.
Shua	שׁוּעַ	Opulence or Cry for Help	The Cana'anite woman Y'hudah took for his concubine.
Shulchan aruch	שֻׁלְחָן עָרוּךְ	Set Table	The code of Jewish law derived from the Talmud.
Sichon	סִיחוֹן	Wiping out, sweeping away.	The king of the Emori/Amorite nation.
Sodom	סְדֹם	Sodom sinful and corrupt	The city in the valley of the Dead Sea, which Adonai destroyed because of its members lack of ethical behaviour.
Sukkot	סֻכֹּת	Tabernacles.	The festival of Tabernacling, a 7-day festival to commemorate Israel's wandering through the wilderness for 40 years – 15 to 21 Tishrei, sometime in late September or early October. This is the third of the three Pilgrimage Festivals.

T

WORD	HEBREW	ENGLISH TRANSLATION	DESCRIPTION
Talmud	תַּלְמוּד	Teaching	The central part of Rabbinic Judaism and the source of Jewish law.
Tamar	תָּמָר	date and date palm	Tamar was Yehudah's daughter-in – law.

WORD	HEBREW	ENGLISH TRANSLATION	DESCRIPTION
Tanakh Acronym for Torah	תּוֹרָה		(5 Books of Moses), Nevi'im (Prophets) and Ketuvim (Writings).
Targum	תִּרְגֹּם		Translation of the Hebrew Bible into aramaic.
Tasria	תַזְרִיעַ	She conceives	Title of the 4th weekly reading of the Book of Leviticus.
Terah	תֶּרַח	Avraham's father.	When Terah died, Adonai spoke with Avram and told him to "Go."
T'rumah/ Terumah	תְּרוּמָה	Gift, offering	The title of the 7th Parashah/weekly reading of the Book of Exodus.
T'tzaveh	פָּרָשָׁה	You shall command	The title of the 8th Parashah/weekly reading of the Book of Exodus.
Thummim	תוּמִים	A stone worn in the breastplate of the Kohen Hagadol.	The thummim was used in the making of decisions to know the advice of Adonai.
Tol'dot	תּוֹלְדוֹת	Generations/History	The weekly parashah focusing on the birth and life of Esav and Ya'akov
Torah	תּוֹרָה	Five books of Moses – Pentateuch	Messianic Jews believe Torah includes all of the Hebrew Bible and the New Covenant.
Thutmoses		dhwty-ms	Born of God Thoth
Tzav	צַו	Give an Order	Title of the 2nd Parashah/weekly reading of the Book of Leviticus
Tzilah	צִלָּה	Shade	Second wife of Lamech and mother of Tubal-Cain.
Tzitzot	צִיצִיֹּת		Knotted ritual fringes/tassels worn by Jewish and Messianic men on an outer garment.
Tzivaot	צבאות	Heavenly army	Used in relation to Adonai Tzivaot, Lord of Hosts.

WORD	HEBREW	ENGLISH TRANSLATION	DESCRIPTION
U			
Urim	אוּרִים	A stone worn in the breastplate of the Kohen Hagadol.	The Urim was used in the making of decisions to know the advice of Adonai.
V			
Va'eira	וָאֵרָא	And I appeared.	The title of the 2nd Weekly Reading in Exodus.
Va'Etchanan	וָאֶתְחַנַּן	Talk about	The title of the 2nd parashah of Deuteronomy
Vayak'hel	וַיַּקְהֵל	He assembled	Title of the 9th weekly reading of the Book of Exodus.
Vayelekh	וַיֵּלֶךְ	Then he went out.	The title of the 9th weekly reading of Deuteronomy.
Vayera	יְרָאֶה	And He appeared.	The title of the 4th weekly reading of Genesis
Vayigash	וַיִּגַּשׁ	He approached	The 11th Parashah of Torah; Ya'akov and his family arrive in Egypt; Yosef confronts his brothers.
Vayikra	וַיִּקְרָא	And He called.	The Hebrew tile of the 3rd Book of Torah, Leviticus, and the 1st Parashah/weekly reading.
Vayishlach	וַיִּשְׁלַח	And he sent	The title of the eight parashah, reading, of Genesis.
Vayechi	וַיְחִי	He lived	Parashah 12 of Genesis.
Va'eira	וַיֵּרָא	And I appeared	The title of the 1st Parashah of the Book of Exodus.
Vayeshev	וַיֵּשֶׁב	He continued living	The story of Yosef's life in Egypt after being sold to Ishmaelite traders

Word	Hebrew	English Translation	Description
Vayetze	וַיֵּצֵא	He went out	Ya'akov travels from his father's home to his uncle's home in Haran, to find a wife.
Vayakheil	וַיַּקְהֵל	And he assembled	The title of the 10th Parashah of the Book of Exodus.
Vayikra	וַיִּקְרָא	And He called	The title of the 3rd Book of the Pentateuch, Torah, Leviticus.
Vayishlach	וַיִּשְׁלַח	He sent	Ya'akov confronts Esav after leaving Lavan's home.
V'ahavta/ Veahavta	וְאָהַבְתָּ	And you shall love.	Prayer recited immediately after the Sh'ma. Found in Deuteronomy 6.
V'Zot HaBrachah	וְזֹאת הַבְּרָכָה	And this is the Blessing.	The 10th and final Parashat of Deuteronomy.

W

X

Y

Word	Hebrew	English Translation	Description
Ya'akov	יַעֲקֹב	He who supplants	Ya'akov supplanted Esav as the first born son and received the fist born's double portion.
Yabok	יַבֹּק		Pouring forth; a river east of the Jordan River; territory of the Ammorites.
Yahweh	יְהֹוָה	Tetragrammaton of Adonai's Name.	Used in many English Bibles.
Y'hoshua	יְהוֹשֻׁעַ	Salvation.	Y'hoshua was with Moshe on Mount Sinai and the leader of Israel, when they crossed the Jordan River into the promised land.

WORD	HEBREW	ENGLISH TRANSLATION	DESCRIPTION
Yarden	יַרְדֵּן	Flowing down.	The Jordan River. The river running along the Jordanian/ Israeli border to the Dead Sea.
Yehudah/Y'hudah	יְהוּדָה	thanksgiving or praise	The fourth son of Ya'akov from Rifka.
Yerushalayim	יְרוּשָׁלַיִם	Foundation of Peace.	The city David captured from the Jebusites. Located in the Southern Levant of Israel on a plateau in the Judean Mountains.
Yeshua	יֵשׁוּעַ	Salvation The Hebrew Name for Jesus	The letter 'J' did not exist before the 15th C. His Name given to Him by Adonai was Yeshua, which means salvation.
Yishma'el	יִשְׁמָעֵאל	God will listen.	The name of Abraham's son through Hagar.
Yishma'elim	יִשְׁמְעָאלִים	God will listen to them.	The group of traders who took Yosef to Egypt.
Yisra'el	יִשְׂרָאֵל	The one who grappled with, Israel	The land given to Avraham, Yitzchak & Ya'akov by Adonai and the name given to Ya'akov by Adonai.
Yitro	יִתְרוֹ	Abundance/plenty Also known as Jethro.	The title of the 5th Parashah of the Book of Exodus, the father-in-law of Moshe.
Yitzchak	יִצְחָק	**Laughter**	Yitzchak was born while Sarah was 90 years old. Sarah laughed at the thought of she and Yitzchak having a child at their age.
Yom Kippur	יוֹם כִּפּוּר		Day of Atonement. Festival held on 10 Tishrei. This is a fasting day of prayer for atonement and release of guilt and shame.
Yom Teruah	יוֹם תְּרוּעָה		Day of Trumpets/shouting/blasting. Festival held on the 1st of Tishrei, the 7th month of the biblical calendar.

Word	Hebrew	English Translation	Description
Yonasan	יְהוֹנָתָן	A portion of the Targum.	Y'honasan was King David's bestfriend, while he was hiding from King Saul.
Yosef	יוֹסֵף		He will add Yosef was the 11th son of Ya'akov, from Rachel. Yosef was sold into slavery by his brothers and became a leading figure in Egypt.

Z

Word	Hebrew	English Translation	Description
Zakar	זָכַר	To remember.	To employ hands, feet and/or lips to do what remembrance requires.
Zakur	זָכוּר	All your males shall appear;	the name of the guide through Sefer HaD'Varim, the Book of Deuteronomy.
Zephaniah	צְפַנְיָה	YHVH has hidden or protected.	Zephaniah was one of the minor prophets of Israel in the 5th Century Israel.
Zevulon/Zebulon	זְבוּלוּן	Resident	Ya'akov's tenth son from Leah.
Zilpah	זִלְפָּה	Fragrant dropping	Leah's servant given to Ya'akov by Leah.
Zipporah	צִפּוֹרָה	bird	The wife of Moshe and the daughter of Yitro.

ABOUT THE AUTHOR

Michael has an extremely strong desire to understand how God works in man's mind and heart. His latest works focus on understanding God's instructions to His children, as outlined in the first 5 books of the Bible. Michael comes to this task with a Masters of Theological Study, a Masters of Education and a PhD in Educational Administration. He has led a group of Messianic believers in Winnipeg, Manitoba and Quebec Canada.